EVERYTHING YOUR FAMILY NEEDS TO KNOW

# MUNEEM KHAATA

## ABH HAR GHAR MUNEEM!!

PERSONAL RECORD KEEPER

# PERSONAL FINANCE LOG

**FINANCE RECORD IN ONE PLACE**

Keeps all the information in one place.

**MAKE IT EASY FOR YOUR LOVED ONES**

**Beneficiary** **Nominee** **Will**

Mishap or death is inevitable & unpredictable

This is one stop solutions to keep record of it all....

**PLAN YOUR FINANCIAL JOURNEY**

**Retirement**

**Assets**

**Liabilities**

Track all of this in your very own way

**BE THE MASTER OF YOUR PERSONAL FINANCE**

Have an upper hand on all your finances

**Keep all the information in one place and keep this book in your locker ONLY to be shared with TRUSTED ones.**

CONCEPT & DESIGN BY AALIYA ZIBRAN INAMDAR

Printed in India

ISBN: 978-93-6045-024-3
First Printing, 2024

Indie Press
A division of Nasadiya Technologies Private Ltd.
Koramangala, Bengaluru
Karnataka-560029

INDIE PRESS PUBLICATIONS.

www.indiepress.in

Edited by Ridham Bassi

Typeset by Nikhil Kamath

Book Cover designed by Ananya

Publishing Consultant - Rechal Fernandes

With all my love,
I dedicate this to my beloved husband, Zibran Inamdar
and my wonderful children, Sami and Haamid Inamdar.

## Foreword

It gives me great pleasure to congratulate Ms. Aaliya Zibran Inamdar, an alumnus of Anjuman-I-Islam's Allana Institute of Management Studies for designing a creative product "Muneem Khaata"

Muneem Khaata is an investment diary that will help you track the progress of your investments over time. It will help you set your financial goals by recording your smallest investments and putting down your thoughts by explaining every investment decision. It will make you more focused and keep you in touch with your monetary decision. Keeping an investment diary over the long term can show you patterns in your thinking and uncover new ideas and strategies for future investments.

As a President of Anjuman-I-Islam, I would like to encourage students of all institutions, we have about 80 institutions under the flagship brand. I take pride in thousands of alumni of Anjuman-I-Islam who are doing good work in thousands of organizations all over the globe and many of them are entrepreneurs. I feel so incredibly fortunate to see so many of my students doing well in their careers.

My Best Wishes to Ms. Aaliya Zibran in her new endeavor.

Padmashree Dr. Zahir Kazi
President
Anjuman-I-Islam

I am proud of my student Aaliya Zibran, whom I taught 15 years back in marketing management. Aaliya's Muneem Khaata is a unique diary for recording investments in FD, mutual funds, jewelry, bonds, houses, land, insurance, and many more financial products. She has used her creativity in designing this unique diary.

Muneem Khaata helps to keep your smallest investment organized, decode balancing your financial portfolio, achieve your financial goals, and helps in recording investment ideas on the go, thus helping you remain stress-free.

I wish my best wishes for launching this unique investment diary, I am sure it will be welcomed by lakhs of consumers from all walks of life.

Prof. Dr. Vidya Hattangadi
Director, Babasaheb Gawde Institute of Management Studies
www.drvidyahattangadi.com

Mrs. Aaliya Zibran Inamdar's passion for making financial management accessible to everyone is truly inspiring. With a deep commitment to simplifying personal finance, she has devoted herself to creating "Muneem Khaata," a planner designed to help individuals manage their finances easily and efficiently. Her dedication to this project is a testament to her belief in the importance of clear, organized financial tracking. Despite managing her responsibilities as a homemaker, Mrs. Inamdar has poured her heart and soul into this planner. Her journey began as a working professional, and she has carried that experience into her role at home, combining her professional skills with her dedication to improving financial management for all. "Muneem Khaata" reflects her thoughtful approach and unwavering commitment. By crafting a tool that integrates all essential financial data into a user-friendly format, she aims to empower individuals—whether they are homemakers, small entrepreneurs, or students—to achieve their financial goals confidently and easily. Mrs. Inamdar's work is a shining example of how passion and dedication can transform everyday challenges into practical solutions for everyone.

Irfan Chikte
Executive Director
Konkan Technical Private Limited

Aaliya Inamdar!!! Congratulation for "Muneem Khaata". You have brought old School way; the written records are back. This has been proven time and again the best way to manage your finances and safeguard your banking details. In current times, financial records are being saved in our laptops and mobiles which are in constant threat of being hacked or data loss.

"Muneem Khaata" is a solution to this threat as it will always be secured in your home, which we all consider to be the safest place on earth. The information will be safe and limited to only those whom you want to share with. Aaliya Inamdar, you have done a wonderful job by making it so organized and detailed not just limiting to financial details but also explaining difficult financial concepts and their importance with so much ease. This will certainly be in my locker with all my details.

Cheers!!! And Best for Luck.

Regards,
Tanveer Inamdar
Co-Founder INDI TECH COATINGS

In today's fast-paced world, managing personal finances can be daunting. From tracking daily expenses to planning for retirement, the complexity of financial management often overwhelms many of us. This is where "Muneem Khaata" steps in—a comprehensive guide designed to simplify and streamline your financial life. Authored by Ms.Aaliya Zibran Inamdar, "Muneem Khaata" covers a wide range of essential topics, including Information Logs, Asset Trackers, Debt Trackers, and Retirement Planning Trackers. Each section is meticulously crafted to provide clear, actionable insights that you can apply immediately to your financial situation. Whether you're looking to keep an accurate record of your assets, manage your debts effectively, or plan for a secure retirement, this book offers practical tools and strategies to help you achieve your goals. What sets "Muneem Khaata" apart is its accessibility. The content is presented straightforwardly, making it easy for anyone—regardless of their financial background—to understand and implement. This book helps you keep track of your current financial status and empowers you to improve your financial health and reach your objectives. I truly believe that "Muneem Khaata" will be an invaluable resource for anyone looking to gain control over their finances. Its comprehensive approach and practical advice make it a must-have for achieving financial stability and success. Your journey towards better financial management begins here, and I am confident that Ms Aaliya Zibran Inamdar's expertise and insights will guide you every step of the way. Enjoy the journey to financial clarity and success with "Muneem Khaata."

Regards,
Vinit Shah
Finance Controller
Adani Port Pvt. Ltd.

Amongst many life skills that go beyond academics and beyond what one learns at school is the skill called financial literacy. It empowers individuals to make informed decisions, fosters financial independence, and ensures a secure future. However, in the Indian context, anything to do with finance and investments is perceived as a specialized skill.

For every little decision about finance and investments, most of us who do not from a background in finance tend to seek advice from specialists or tend to take a very conservative approach and follow our elders or family members who invested in traditional asset classes like gold, term deposits in banks or real estate.

Moreover, while every middle-class Indian family may have savings and investments in asset classes – traditional or modern, rare are those who maintain collated and compiled records of their investments or liabilities – a record that they can refer to, to analyze how the assets are performing or even as a legacy document that can serve their next generation to know what they have inherited.

While these are the gaps in financial management in the Indian context, can there be a document that can help you become more financially aware and at the same time serve as a logbook of your assets, investments, liabilities, and financial commitments? Aaliya Inamdar has an answer.

This painstakingly designed journal that you hold in your hands is the answer. Primarily this is a financial planning journal that helps you list out all your investments and liabilities in the Indian context – be it term deposits, gold, mutual funds, equity or insurance or even your EMIs, loans outgo, or credit card payment cycles – this book offers valuable insights and practical tools tailored to the unique financial environment of India. It emphasizes the importance of traditional wisdom while integrating modern financial practices, ensuring that you can make the best use of both worlds. Whether you are a student, a young professional, a homemaker, or someone approaching retirement, this logbook aims to demystify the world of finance.

Aptly called – Muneem Khaata, designed beautifully to last for a decade or more, this will be your trusted companion to become financially secure and help you improve your investment decisions. Not only that but this logbook also serves as a legacy document that you pass on from one generation to another, ensuring that after you, your next generation is not left ignorant of your life's financial accomplishments and what they have inherited. The author, a seasoned marketing professional has a passion for financial education and has crafted a resource that is both informative and inspiring. She has a genuine desire to empower individuals to take control of their financial destinies. Aaliya's approachable style and clarity of thought about even the most complex topics ensures that you, regardless of your financial background, can benefit from this book.

I congratulate Aaliya on her remarkable achievement and wish her all the success as she embarks on this journey as an author. And for readers – I wish you make the most of Aaliya's hard work to make your life journey easier.

Sincerely,
Sadiq H. Kazi,
President, The Education Society, Kadwai.
CEO, Muddyboots Retails Pvt Ltd.
Founder, Umalti Pruthvi Foundation

Dear all,
In an age where books can be found at the swipe of a screen or the click of a button, it is a rare and precious thing to come across a work that resonates deeply, speaks to the heart, and stays with you long after the last page is turned. The book you hold in your hands, Muneem Khaata, is one such treasure.

Through its pages, you will embark on a new, well-planned financial journey. Ms. Aaliya Inamdar's ability to bring all the important financial aspects one must know within a family is nothing short of extraordinary, and I hope that you, dear reader, will find as much joy in reading it and using it for as long as a decade as I will.

Muneem Khaata is more than a financial logbook. It is a guide to understanding and planning for the future, a thoughtful companion on the road to financial freedom. Whether you're laying the groundwork for your retirement plan or simply seeking to organize your financial life, this book offers invaluable insights and tools.

As you turn the pages, take a moment to appreciate the artistry and heart that have brought this book to life. It is a gift to us all, a reminder of the enduring power of writing to pass on our legacy, inspiring us to take control of our finances and take one step towards achieving financial goals.

Enjoy the journey.

S. M. Sheikh
Chartered Accountant

# THIS IS ME

**Full Name:**

**Contact Number:**

**Email ID:**

**Address:**

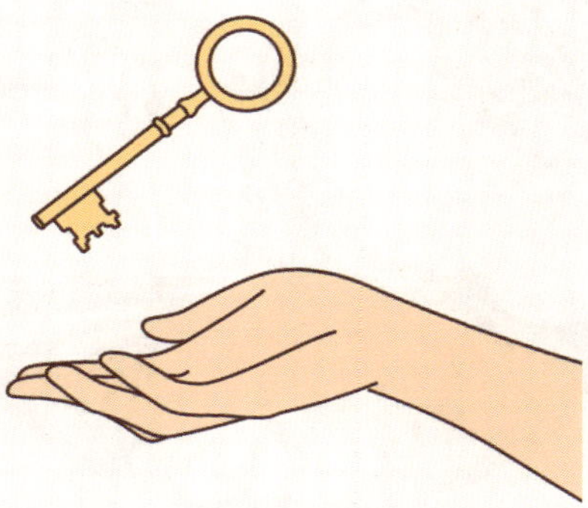

# AND THIS IS MY LEGACY

# FAMILY MEMBERS INFORMATION

## NAMES OF FAMILY MEMBERS

| No. | COUPLE NAME | DEPENDENT CHILDREN | DEPENDENT PARENTS |
|---|---|---|---|
| 1 | | | |
| 2 | | | |
| 3 | | | |
| 4 | | | |

# FAMILY INFORMATION DOCUMENT

| No. | PARTICULARS | NAME | MOBILE | EMAIL |
|---|---|---|---|---|
| 1 | SELF | | | |
| 2 | SPOUSE | | | |
| 3 | NAANI | | | |
| 4 | NAANA | | | |
| 5 | DAADI | | | |
| 6 | DAADA | | | |
| 7 | CHILD 1 | | | |
| 8 | CHILD 2 | | | |
| 9 | | | | |
| 10 | | | | |

*Home Address*

*Parents Address*

*In-Laws Address*

# TERMS IN FINANCE

**BUDGETING**
The process of creating a plan to manage income and expenses over a specific period, usually on a monthly or yearly basis.

**GST**
GST is a single tax on the supply of goods and services, right from the manufacturer to the consumer.

**SAVING**
Savings are income not spent, reserved for future needs or emergencies, held in forms like savings accounts, fixed deposits, or investments.

**INVESTMENT**
Investment involves directing funds or resources towards an opportunity, like purchasing stocks or real estate etc., in anticipation of generating a profit or income in the long run.

**ROI**
Return on Investment (ROI) is a performance measure used to evaluate the efficiency or profitability of an investment. A higher ROI indicates that the investment gains compare favorably to its cost.

**ROI= (Net Return/ Investment cost)*100 = ROI %**

**CREDIT SCORE**
A credit score is a 3-digit number between 300 and 900, generated by credit bureaus like CIBIL, that reflects an individual's creditworthiness based on their past credit behavior and repayment history. A higher score indicates better creditworthiness, which can influence the approval of loans or credit cards.

**RATE OF INTEREST**
The interest rate is the percentage of the principal that a lender charges a borrower, usually expressed as an annual percentage rate (APR).

**EMI**
EMI, or Equated Monthly Installment, is a fixed monthly payment made by a borrower to a lender to repay both the principal and interest of a loan within a set timeframe. It's used to pay off both the principal and interest components of an outstanding loan within a given time frame.

**UPI**
Unified Payments Interface (UPI) is an instant payment system developed by NPCI allowing users to transfer money between bank accounts via smartphone apps without entering bank details, regulated by RBI.

**AADHAAR CARD**
Aadhaar is a 12-digit unique identification number issued by the Unique Identification Authority of India on behalf of the Government of India. It serves as a proof of identity and address for residents of India and not a proof of citizenship. The Aadhaar number is unique for each individual and is based on their biometrics and demographic data.

**PAN CARD**
A PAN card, or Permanent Account Number card, is a 10-digit alphanumeric identifier issued by the Indian Income Tax Department. It serves as a unique identifier for tax-paying entities in India, helping to track and manage their financial transactions.

*Alert: This above information is for your knowledge, kindly do your own research.

# FINANCIAL PLANNING

Process of getting your Finance Organized

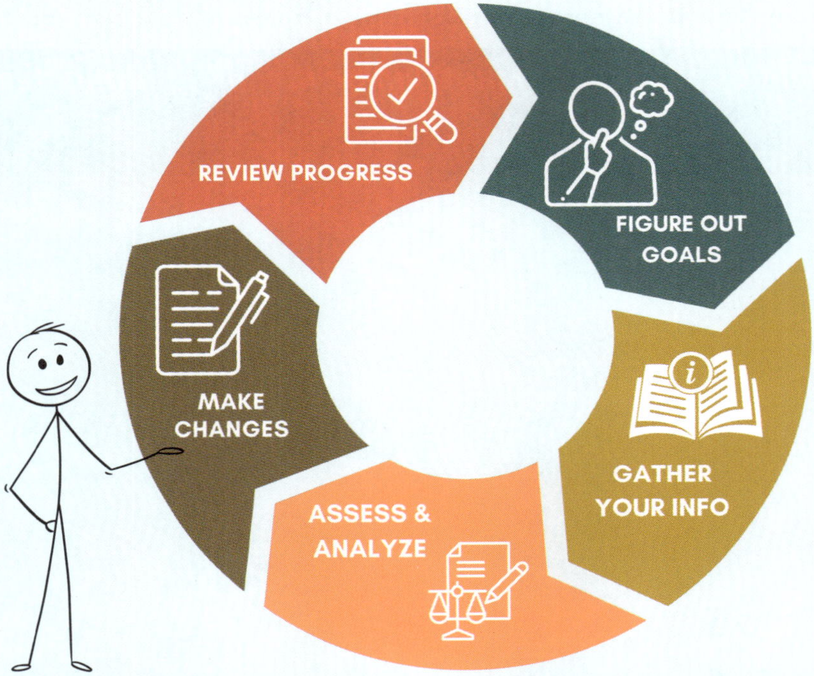


## BENEFITS

- **Goal setting:** It helps you track your financial goals.
- **Achieving financial goals:** Set short term, mid-term and long-term goals.
- **Expenses:** It helps you track your Income & expenses in one place.
- **Managing Debts:** It allows to maximize savings by keeping a track of debts.
- **Retirement Planning:** This must be one of your long-term financial goals.
- **Minimizing taxes:** By investing in tax free schemes or consulting your financial advisor for the same.
- **Financial security:** Having a financial plan gives you the sense of security.
- **Improved standard of living:** A financial plan improves your standard of living by saving on taxes, making wise investments, tracking expenses, and growing wealth.
- **A written financial plan increases confidence.**

"Financial freedom is available to those who learn about it and work for it." - Robert Kiyosaki

Disclaimer: This page is purely for educational purposes only. And not a financial advisory.

# GOAL SETTING

## Personal Finance

Use this table to define your short-term, mid-term and long-term personal goals. Make sure your goals are (Specific, Measurable, Achievable, Relevant, and Time-bound) **SMART**.

| SHORT-TERM GOAL (1-24 MONTHS) | MID-TERM GOAL (2-5 YEARS) | LONG-TERM GOAL (5-10 YEARS) |
|---|---|---|
| | | |
| | | |
| | | |
| | | |
| | | |

"Setting goals is the first step in turning the invisible into the visible."

# SETTING ACTIONS FOR YOUR GOALS >>>

ACTION PLAN

**SHORT TERM**

ACTION PLAN

**MID TERM**

ACTION PLAN

**LONG TERM**

"The path to success is to take massive, determined action."

# FINANCIAL GOALS CHECKLIST

- Build an Emergency Fund
- Boost a Low Credit Score
- Generate passive income
- Pay your debt ASAP
- Save for Retirement
- Appoint a nominee for every asset
- Keep a track of your personal finances
- Teach kids about money from early age, age appropriately.
- Priotorize your health
- Make your personal balance sheet
- Have a diversified portfolio
- Keep some funds handy
- Invest in yourself
- Automate Investing & Savings
- Increase your money knowledge
- Keep record of all your debts
- Invest in sinking fund
- Discuss money with your family & children
- Set healthy boundaries with money (Avoid unnecessary expenses)
- Consider sharing financial information with at least one trusted family member.
- Keep evaluating your investments from time to time
- Invest in mutual funds at an early age (Learn about its benefits, secrets which no one will tell)

# WHAT IS A PERSONAL BALANCE SHEET?

Your personal balance sheet is a document that gives you a clear look at three aspects of your finances: assets, liabilities and net worth.

## PERSONAL BALANCE SHEET CATEGORIES

### ASSETS

- Retirement Account
- Savings Account
- Gold
- Investment account

–

### LIABILITIES

- Loan debt
- Credit Card Debt
- Medical Debt

=

### NET WORTH

Your **net worth** is an overall look at what you own minus what you owe.

@theindianplanner

## WHY SHOULD YOU MAKE A PERSONAL BALANCE SHEET?

Track Interest Rates on all your outstanding debts

Define high-debt areas to create targeted repayment strategies.

Protect your assets

Understand your overall financial situations before making big decisions

@theindianplanner

# GOAL SETTING

## Personal Finance

Use this table to define your short-term, mid-term and long-term personal goals. Make sure your goals are (Specific, Measurable, Achievable, Relevant, and Time-bound) **SMART**.

| SHORT-TERM GOAL<br>(1-24 MONTHS) | MID-TERM GOAL<br>(2-5 YEARS) | LONG-TERM GOAL<br>(5-10 YEARS) |
|---|---|---|
| | | |
| | | |
| | | |
| | | |
| | | |

"Setting goals is the first step in turning the invisible into the visible." - Anonymous

# SETTING ACTIONS FOR YOUR GOALS >>>

ACTION PLAN

**SHORT TERM**

ACTION PLAN

**MID TERM**

ACTION PLAN

**LONG TERM**

"The path to success is to take massive, determined action." - Anonymous

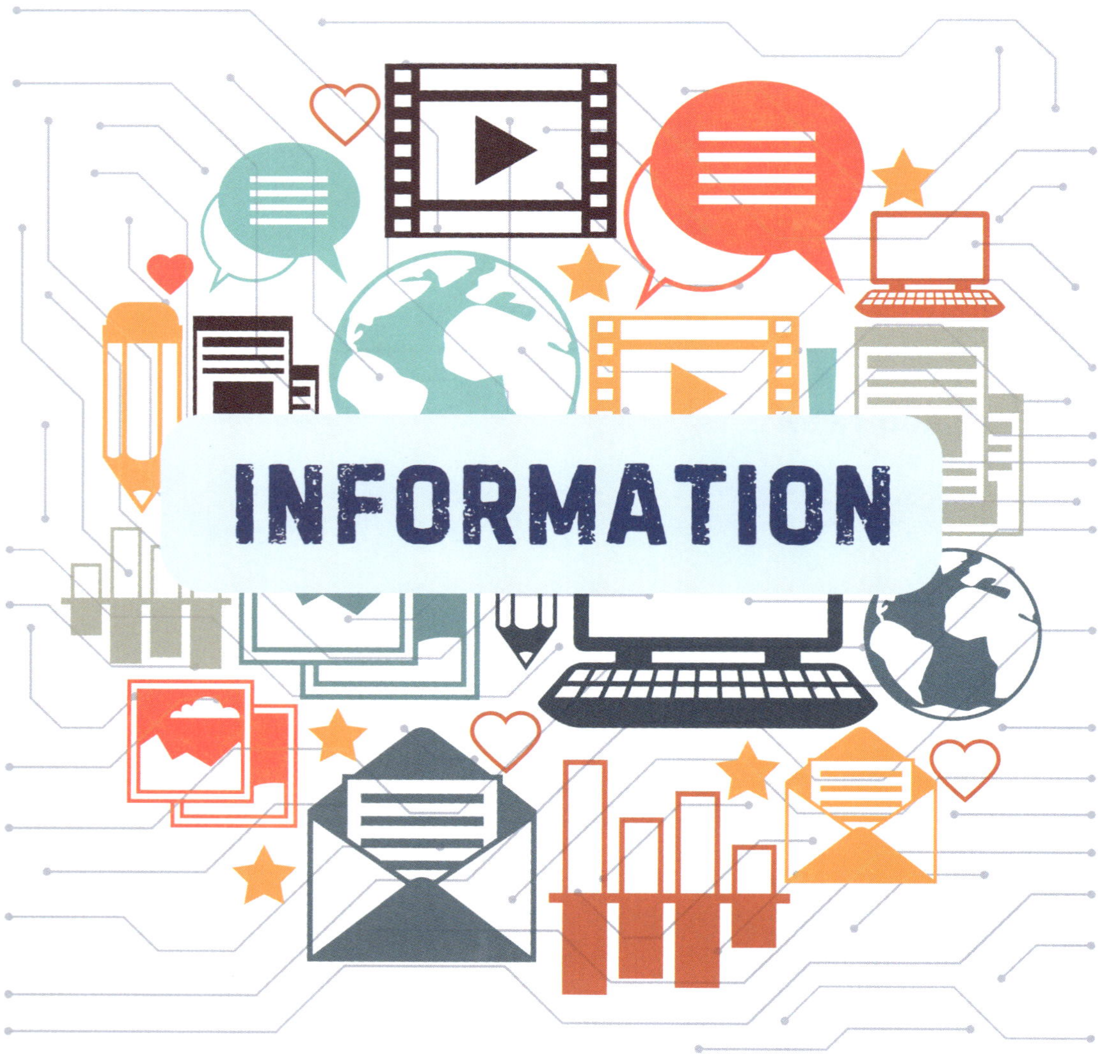
INFORMATION

# IMPORTANT CONTACTS

**Lawyer**

NAME
PHONE
EMAIL
ADDRESS

**Bank Manager**

NAME
PHONE
EMAIL
ADDRESS

**Doctor**

NAME
PHONE
EMAIL
ADDRESS

**Chartered Accountant**

NAME
PHONE
EMAIL
ADDRESS

**Financial Advisor**

NAME
PHONE
EMAIL
ADDRESS

**Insurance Advisor**

NAME
PHONE
EMAIL
ADDRESS

NAME
PHONE
EMAIL
ADDRESS

NAME
PHONE
EMAIL
ADDRESS

NAME
PHONE
EMAIL
ADDRESS

NAME
PHONE
EMAIL
ADDRESS

"Coming together is a beginning, staying together is progress, and working together is success." - Henry Ford

# IMPORTANT CONTACTS

NAME
PHONE
EMAIL
ADDRESS

NAME
PHONE
EMAIL
ADDRESS

NAME
PHONE
EMAIL
ADDRESS

NAME
PHONE
EMAIL
ADDRESS

NAME
PHONE
EMAIL
ADDRESS

NAME
PHONE
EMAIL
ADDRESS

NAME
PHONE
EMAIL
ADDRESS

NAME
PHONE
EMAIL
ADDRESS

NAME
PHONE
EMAIL
ADDRESS

NAME
PHONE
EMAIL
ADDRESS

"It is the long history of humankind (and animal kind, too) that those who learned to collaborate and improvise most effectively have prevailed." - Charles Darwin

# IMPORTANT CONTACTS

NAME
PHONE
EMAIL
ADDRESS

NAME
PHONE
EMAIL
ADDRESS

NAME
PHONE
EMAIL
ADDRESS

NAME
PHONE
EMAIL
ADDRESS

NAME
PHONE
EMAIL
ADDRESS

NAME
PHONE
EMAIL
ADDRESS

NAME
PHONE
EMAIL
ADDRESS

NAME
PHONE
EMAIL
ADDRESS

NAME
PHONE
EMAIL
ADDRESS

NAME
PHONE
EMAIL
ADDRESS

"Find a group of people who challenge and inspire you, spend a lot of time with them, and it will change your life." - Amy Poehler

# IMPORTANT DOCUMENTS

Adult

**NAME OF DOCUMENTS HOLDER:** ______________________________

| No. | DOCUMENT | DOCUMENT NUMBER | DOC LOCATION PHYSICAL | DOC LOCATION VIRTUAL | EXPIRY |
|---|---|---|---|---|---|
| 1 | PAN CARD | | | | |
| 2 | PASSPORT | | | | |
| 3 | AADHAAR CARD | | | | |
| 4 | DRIVING LICENSE | | | | |
| 5 | ELECTION CARD | | | | |
| 6 | WILL | | | | |
| 7 | BIRTH CERTIFICATE | | | | |
| 8 | MARRIAGE CERTIFICATE | | | | |
| 9 | LOCKER KEY | | | | |
| 10 | INSURANCE | | | | |
| 11 | PROPERTY PAPERS | | | | |
| 12 | HOME LOAN DOC | | | | |
| 13 | OTHER LOAN DOC | | | | |
| 14 | INCOME TAX RETURNS | | | | |
| 15 | INVESTMENT DOC | | | | |
| 16 | MEDICLAIM DOC | | | | |
| 17 | | | | | |
| 18 | | | | | |
| 19 | | | | | |
| 20 | | | | | |

*Notes* ..............................................

..............................................

..............................................

..............................................

"Wealth is not his that has it, but his that enjoys it." - Andy Warhol

# IMPORTANT DOCUMENTS

Adult

**NAME OF DOCUMENTS HOLDER:** ____________________

| No. | DOCUMENT | DOCUMENT NUMBER | DOC LOCATION PHYSICAL | VIRTUAL | EXPIRY |
|---|---|---|---|---|---|
| 1 | PAN CARD | | | | |
| 2 | PASSPORT | | | | |
| 3 | AADHAAR CARD | | | | |
| 4 | DRIVING LICENSE | | | | |
| 5 | ELECTION CARD | | | | |
| 6 | WILL | | | | |
| 7 | BIRTH CERTIFICATE | | | | |
| 8 | MARRIAGE CERTIFICATE | | | | |
| 9 | LOCKER KEY | | | | |
| 10 | INSURANCE | | | | |
| 11 | PROPERTY PAPERS | | | | |
| 12 | HOME LOAN DOC | | | | |
| 13 | OTHER LOAN DOC | | | | |
| 14 | INCOME TAX RETURNS | | | | |
| 15 | INVESTMENT DOC | | | | |
| 16 | MEDICLAIM DOC | | | | |
| 17 | | | | | |
| 18 | | | | | |
| 19 | | | | | |
| 20 | | | | | |

*Notes* ....................................................

....................................................

....................................................

....................................................

"Make sure you have financial intelligence; I don't care if you have money or you don't have money. You need to go and study finance no matter what." - Daymond John

# IMPORTANT DOCUMENTS

Adult

**NAME OF DOCUMENTS HOLDER:** ______________________________

| No. | DOCUMENT | DOCUMENT NUMBER | DOC LOCATION PHYSICAL | DOC LOCATION VIRTUAL | EXPIRY |
|---|---|---|---|---|---|
| 1 | PAN CARD | | | | |
| 2 | PASSPORT | | | | |
| 3 | AADHAAR CARD | | | | |
| 4 | DRIVING LICENSE | | | | |
| 5 | ELECTION CARD | | | | |
| 6 | WILL | | | | |
| 7 | BIRTH CERTIFICATE | | | | |
| 8 | MARRIAGE CERTIFICATE | | | | |
| 9 | LOCKER KEY | | | | |
| 10 | INSURANCE | | | | |
| 11 | PROPERTY PAPERS | | | | |
| 12 | HOME LOAN DOC | | | | |
| 13 | OTHER LOAN DOC | | | | |
| 14 | INCOME TAX RETURNS | | | | |
| 15 | INVESTMENT DOC | | | | |
| 16 | MEDICLAIM DOC | | | | |
| 17 | | | | | |
| 18 | | | | | |
| 19 | | | | | |
| 20 | | | | | |

*Notes* ..............................................................

..............................................................

..............................................................

..............................................................

"Tough times never last, but tough people do." - Robert H. Schuller

# IMPORTANT DOCUMENTS

Adult

**NAME OF DOCUMENTS HOLDER:** ____________________

| No. | DOCUMENT | DOCUMENT NUMBER | DOC LOCATION PHYSICAL | DOC LOCATION VIRTUAL | EXPIRY |
|---|---|---|---|---|---|
| 1 | PAN CARD | | | | |
| 2 | PASSPORT | | | | |
| 3 | AADHAAR CARD | | | | |
| 4 | DRIVING LICENSE | | | | |
| 5 | ELECTION CARD | | | | |
| 6 | WILL | | | | |
| 7 | BIRTH CERTIFICATE | | | | |
| 8 | MARRIAGE CERTIFICATE | | | | |
| 9 | LOCKER KEY | | | | |
| 10 | INSURANCE | | | | |
| 11 | PROPERTY PAPERS | | | | |
| 12 | HOME LOAN DOC | | | | |
| 13 | OTHER LOAN DOC | | | | |
| 14 | INCOME TAX RETURNS | | | | |
| 15 | INVESTMENT DOC | | | | |
| 16 | MEDICLAIM DOC | | | | |
| 17 | | | | | |
| 18 | | | | | |
| 19 | | | | | |
| 20 | | | | | |

*Notes* ....................

....................

....................

....................

"Making money is art and working is art and good business is the best art." - Ayn Rand

# IMPORTANT DOCUMENTS

Child

**NAME OF DOCUMENTS HOLDER:** ______________________________

| No. | DOCUMENT | DOCUMENT NUMBER | DOC LOCATION PHYSICAL | VIRTUAL | EXPIRY |
|---|---|---|---|---|---|
| 1 | PAN CARD | | | | |
| 2 | PASSPORT | | | | |
| 3 | AADHAAR CARD | | | | |
| 4 | DRIVING LICENSE | | | | |
| 5 | ELECTION CARD | | | | |
| 6 | WILL | | | | |
| 7 | BIRTH CERTIFICATE | | | | |
| 8 | MARRIAGE CERTIFICATE | | | | |
| 9 | LOCKER KEY | | | | |
| 10 | INSURANCE | | | | |
| 11 | PROPERTY PAPERS | | | | |
| 12 | HOME LOAN DOC | | | | |
| 13 | OTHER LOAN DOC | | | | |
| 14 | INCOME TAX RETURNS | | | | |
| 15 | INVESTMENT DOC | | | | |
| 16 | MEDICLAIM DOC | | | | |
| 17 | | | | | |
| 18 | | | | | |
| 19 | | | | | |
| 20 | | | | | |

*Notes* ..............................................

..............................................

..............................................

..............................................

"I find that the harder I work, the more luck I seem to have." - Thomas Jefferson

# IMPORTANT DOCUMENTS

Child

**NAME OF DOCUMENTS HOLDER:** ____________________

| No. | DOCUMENT | DOCUMENT NUMBER | DOC LOCATION PHYSICAL | VIRTUAL | EXPIRY |
|---|---|---|---|---|---|
| 1 | PAN CARD | | | | |
| 2 | PASSPORT | | | | |
| 3 | AADHAAR CARD | | | | |
| 4 | DRIVING LICENSE | | | | |
| 5 | ELECTION CARD | | | | |
| 6 | WILL | | | | |
| 7 | BIRTH CERTIFICATE | | | | |
| 8 | MARRIAGE CERTIFICATE | | | | |
| 9 | LOCKER KEY | | | | |
| 10 | INSURANCE | | | | |
| 11 | PROPERTY PAPERS | | | | |
| 12 | HOME LOAN DOC | | | | |
| 13 | OTHER LOAN DOC | | | | |
| 14 | INCOME TAX RETURNS | | | | |
| 15 | INVESTMENT DOC | | | | |
| 16 | MEDICLAIM DOC | | | | |
| 17 | | | | | |
| 18 | | | | | |
| 19 | | | | | |
| 20 | | | | | |

*Notes* ....................

"The biggest challenge after success is shutting up about it." - Criss Jami

# LOCKER DETAILS

ACCOUNT HOLDER

BANK NAME

ACCOUNT NUMBER

LOCKER NO.

NOMINEE

REMARKS

ACCOUNT HOLDER

BANK NAME

ACCOUNT NUMBER

LOCKER NO.

NOMINEE

REMARKS

ACCOUNT HOLDER

BANK NAME

ACCOUNT NUMBER

LOCKER NO.

NOMINEE

REMARKS

ACCOUNT HOLDER

BANK NAME

ACCOUNT NUMBER

LOCKER NO.

NOMINEE

REMARKS

*Notes*

"Being Rich is having money, being wealthy is having time" - Margaret Bonnano

# FIN PASSWORD TRACKER

URL *Bank website*
CUSTOMER ID:
PASSWORD:
TPIN:
CONTACT:
EMAIL ID:
OTHER INFO:

URL *Insurance Company*
CUSTOMER ID:
PASSWORD:
TPIN:
CONTACT:
EMAIL ID:
OTHER INFO:

URL
CUSTOMER ID:
PASSWORD:
TPIN:
CONTACT:
EMAIL ID:
OTHER INFO:

URL
CUSTOMER ID:
PASSWORD:
TPIN:
CONTACT:
EMAIL ID:
OTHER INFO:

URL
CUSTOMER ID:
PASSWORD:
TPIN:
CONTACT:
EMAIL ID:
OTHER INFO:

URL
CUSTOMER ID:
PASSWORD:
TPIN:
CONTACT:
EMAIL ID:
OTHER INFO:

URL
CUSTOMER ID:
PASSWORD:
TPIN:
CONTACT:
EMAIL ID:
OTHER INFO:

URL
CUSTOMER ID:
PASSWORD:
TPIN:
CONTACT:
EMAIL ID:
OTHER INFO:

*Notes*

**Pro Tip:** Write your passwords in pencil & keep changing them ones in every three months for safety purpose.

# FIN PASSWORD TRACKER

**URL**

CUSTOMER ID:

PASSWORD:

TPIN:

CONTACT:

EMAIL ID:

OTHER INFO:

**URL**

CUSTOMER ID:

PASSWORD:

TPIN:

CONTACT:

EMAIL ID:

OTHER INFO:

**URL**

CUSTOMER ID:

PASSWORD:

TPIN:

CONTACT:

EMAIL ID:

OTHER INFO:

**URL**

CUSTOMER ID:

PASSWORD:

TPIN:

CONTACT:

EMAIL ID:

OTHER INFO:

**URL**

CUSTOMER ID:

PASSWORD:

TPIN:

CONTACT:

EMAIL ID:

OTHER INFO:

**URL**

CUSTOMER ID:

PASSWORD:

TPIN:

CONTACT:

EMAIL ID:

OTHER INFO:

**URL**

CUSTOMER ID:

PASSWORD:

TPIN:

CONTACT:

EMAIL ID:

OTHER INFO:

**URL**

CUSTOMER ID:

PASSWORD:

TPIN:

CONTACT:

EMAIL ID:

OTHER INFO:

*Notes*

**Pro Tip:** Write your passwords in pencil & keep changing them ones in every three months for safety purpose.

# FIN PASSWORD TRACKER

**URL**
CUSTOMER ID:
PASSWORD:
TPIN:
CONTACT:
EMAIL ID:
OTHER INFO:

**URL**
CUSTOMER ID:
PASSWORD:
TPIN:
CONTACT:
EMAIL ID:
OTHER INFO:

**URL**
CUSTOMER ID:
PASSWORD:
TPIN:
CONTACT:
EMAIL ID:
OTHER INFO:

**URL**
CUSTOMER ID:
PASSWORD:
TPIN:
CONTACT:
EMAIL ID:
OTHER INFO:

**URL**
CUSTOMER ID:
PASSWORD:
TPIN:
CONTACT:
EMAIL ID:
OTHER INFO:

**URL**
CUSTOMER ID:
PASSWORD:
TPIN:
CONTACT:
EMAIL ID:
OTHER INFO:

**URL**
CUSTOMER ID:
PASSWORD:
TPIN:
CONTACT:
EMAIL ID:
OTHER INFO:

**URL**
CUSTOMER ID:
PASSWORD:
TPIN:
CONTACT:
EMAIL ID:
OTHER INFO:

*Notes*

**Pro Tip:** Write your passwords in pencil & keep changing them ones in every three months for safety purpose.

# SUBSCRIPTION TRACKER

**URL** Tickertape

**USERNAME:**

**PASSWORD:**

**CONTACT:**

**EMAIL LINKED:**

**EXPIRATION DATE:**

**OTHER INFO:**

**URL**

**USERNAME:**

**PASSWORD:**

**CONTACT:**

**EMAIL LINKED:**

**EXPIRATION DATE:**

**OTHER INFO:**

**URL**

**USERNAME:**

**PASSWORD:**

**CONTACT:**

**EMAIL LINKED:**

**EXPIRATION DATE:**

**OTHER INFO:**

**URL**

**USERNAME:**

**PASSWORD:**

**CONTACT:**

**EMAIL LINKED:**

**EXPIRATION DATE:**

**OTHER INFO:**

**URL**

**USERNAME:**

**PASSWORD:**

**CONTACT:**

**EMAIL LINKED:**

**EXPIRATION DATE:**

**OTHER INFO:**

**URL**

**USERNAME:**

**PASSWORD:**

**CONTACT:**

**EMAIL LINKED:**

**EXPIRATION DATE:**

**OTHER INFO:**

**URL**

**USERNAME:**

**PASSWORD:**

**CONTACT:**

**EMAIL LINKED:**

**EXPIRATION DATE:**

**OTHER INFO:**

**URL**

**USERNAME:**

**PASSWORD:**

**CONTACT:**

**EMAIL LINKED:**

**EXPIRATION DATE:**

**OTHER INFO:**

*Notes*

**Pro Tip:** Write your passwords in pencil & keep changing them ones in every three months for safety purpose.

# SUBSCRIPTION TRACKER

**URL**

USERNAME:

PASSWORD:

CONTACT:

EMAIL LINKED:

EXPIRATION DATE:

OTHER INFO:

**URL**

USERNAME:

PASSWORD:

CONTACT:

EMAIL LINKED:

EXPIRATION DATE:

OTHER INFO:

**URL**

USERNAME:

PASSWORD:

CONTACT:

EMAIL LINKED:

EXPIRATION DATE:

OTHER INFO:

**URL**

USERNAME:

PASSWORD:

CONTACT:

EMAIL LINKED:

EXPIRATION DATE:

OTHER INFO:

**URL**

USERNAME:

PASSWORD:

CONTACT:

EMAIL LINKED:

EXPIRATION DATE:

OTHER INFO:

**URL**

USERNAME:

PASSWORD:

CONTACT:

EMAIL LINKED:

EXPIRATION DATE:

OTHER INFO:

**URL**

USERNAME:

PASSWORD:

CONTACT:

EMAIL LINKED:

EXPIRATION DATE:

OTHER INFO:

**URL**

USERNAME:

PASSWORD:

CONTACT:

EMAIL LINKED:

EXPIRATION DATE:

OTHER INFO:

*Notes*

**Pro Tip:** Write your passwords in pencil & keep changing them ones in every three months for safety purpose.

# VEHICLE INFORMATION

**VEHICLE NAME:**

REGISTERING AUTHORITY: (RTO) ____________________

TYPE OF VEHICLE: ____________________

REGISTRATION NO: ____________________ REG DATE: ____________________

CHASSIS NO: ____________________ ENGINE NO: ____________________

OWNER NAME.: ____________________ CONTACT ____________________

VEHICLE CLASS: ____________________ FUEL: ____________________

MAKER/ MODEL: ____________________

FITNESS/REGN UPTO: ____________________ MV TAX UPTO: ____________________

EMISSION NORMS: ____________________ RC STATUS: ____________________

REGN ADDRESS: ____________________

INSURANCE DETAILS: ____________________ INSURANCE VALIDITY: ____________________

NOTES/ EXTRA INFO: ____________________

____________________

**VEHICLE NAME:**

REGISTERING AUTHORITY: (RTO) ____________________

TYPE OF VEHICLE: ____________________

REGISTRATION NO: ____________________ REG DATE: ____________________

CHASSIS NO: ____________________ ENGINE NO: ____________________

OWNER NAME.: ____________________ CONTACT ____________________

VEHICLE CLASS: ____________________ FUEL: ____________________

MAKER/ MODEL: ____________________

FITNESS/REGN UPTO: ____________________ MV TAX UPTO: ____________________

EMISSION NORMS: ____________________ RC STATUS: ____________________

REGN ADDRESS: ____________________

INSURANCE DETAILS: ____________________ INSURANCE VALIDITY: ____________________

NOTES/ EXTRA INFO: ____________________

____________________

"Spending money is much more difficult than making money." - Jack Ma

# VEHICLE INFORMATION

**VEHICLE NAME:**

REGISTERING AUTHORITY: (RTO) ____________________

TYPE OF VEHICLE: ____________________

REGISTRATION NO: ____________ REG DATE: ____________

CHASSIS NO: ____________ ENGINE NO: ____________

OWNER NAME.: ____________ CONTACT ____________

VEHICLE CLASS: ____________ FUEL: ____________

MAKER/ MODEL: ____________________

FITNESS/REGN UPTO: ____________ MV TAX UPTO: ____________

EMISSION NORMS: ____________ RC STATUS: ____________

REGN ADDRESS: ____________________

INSURANCE DETAILS: ____________ INSURANCE VALIDITY: ____________

NOTES/ EXTRA INFO: ____________________

**VEHICLE NAME:**

REGISTERING AUTHORITY: (RTO) ____________________

TYPE OF VEHICLE: ____________________

REGISTRATION NO: ____________ REG DATE: ____________

CHASSIS NO: ____________ ENGINE NO: ____________

OWNER NAME.: ____________ CONTACT ____________

VEHICLE CLASS: ____________ FUEL: ____________

MAKER/ MODEL: ____________________

FITNESS/REGN UPTO: ____________ MV TAX UPTO: ____________

EMISSION NORMS: ____________ RC STATUS: ____________

REGN ADDRESS: ____________________

INSURANCE DETAILS: ____________ INSURANCE VALIDITY: ____________

NOTES/ EXTRA INFO: ____________________

"Wealth is far away, poverty is close at hand."- Ancient Sumerian proverb

# ABOUT INDIAN BANKS

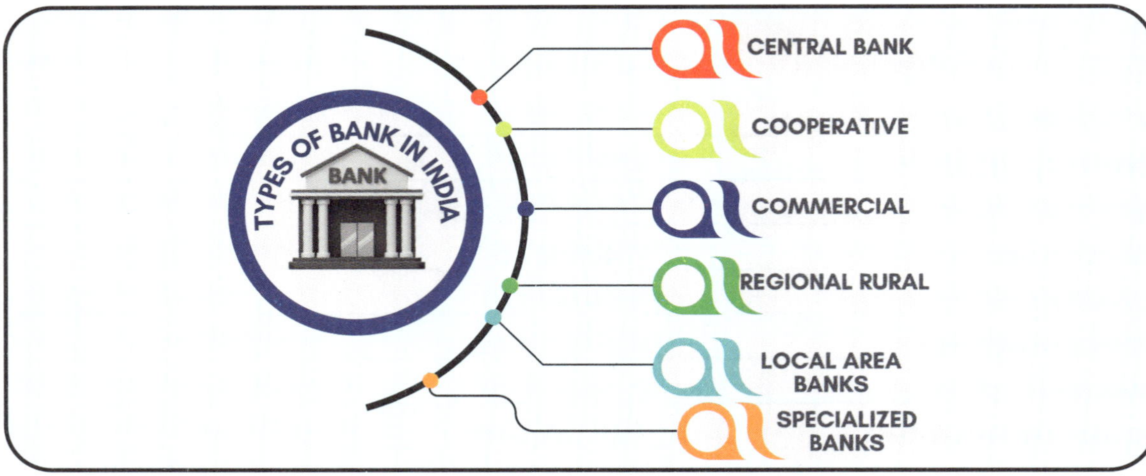

## CENTRAL BANK

A country has only one central bank, and in India we call it the ***Reserve Bank of India*** or RBI. The **RBI** issues rules and regulations for each bank as a means to monitor the activities of all banks in the country.

## COOPERATIVE BANK

A cooperative bank is a small financial institution where members are both owners and customers. Regulated by the RBI and registered under the States Cooperative Societies Act.

## COMMERCIAL BANK

A commercial bank is a financial institution that handles money-related operations for the public, offers investment loans, and seeks profit.

## REGIONAL RURAL BANK

Regional Rural Banks (RRBs) in India are government banks operating at a regional level, providing basic banking and financial services primarily to rural areas.

## LOCAL AREA BANK

Local area banks are small private banks operating in rural and semi-urban areas with limited financial services within a specific geographic area.

## SPECIALIZED BANK

Some banks like EXIM Bank, SIDBI, and NABARD specialize in meeting specific business needs and support businesses in particular sectors are called specialized banks.

## FOREIGN BANK

Foreign banks provide financial services to international customers abroad, while foreign bank branches abide by regulations from both their home and host countries.

# INDIAN BANKS ACCOUNTS

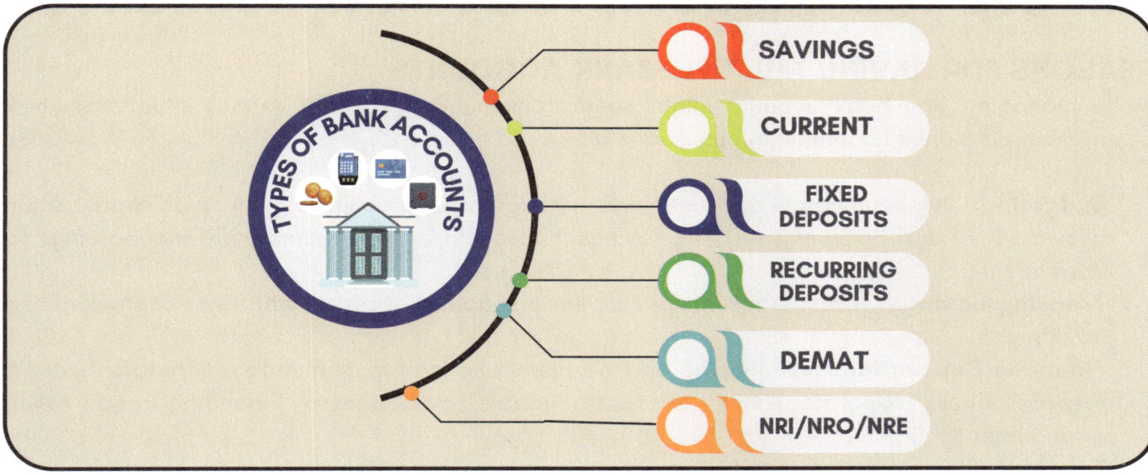


## SAVINGS ACCOUNT

It is the most basic type of account you can open at any bank. A savings account provides a safe place to deposit money with the bank and allows for easy withdrawals when needed.

## CURRENT ACCOUNT

Businessmen with frequent transactions open current bank accounts for deposits, withdrawals, and contra transactions.

## FIXED DEPOSITS

Opening a Fixed Deposit account with a bank allows you to earn guaranteed interest on deposited sums for a specific period, offering higher returns compared to a Savings Account.

## RECURRING DEPOSITS

A recurring deposit account is a financial account held in a bank or post office, where the account holder deposits a fixed amount of money monthly for a specified duration, typically lasting from one to five years.

## DEMAT ACCOUNT

A Demat Account stores details about your shares and securities, transforming your investments into a digital format, eliminating the necessity for paper records.

## NRO & NRE ACCOUNT

An **NRE** account allows transferring foreign earnings to India in rupees, while an **NRO** account manages income earned in India by an NRI in rupees, including pension, rental, and dividend income.

# SHOULD YOU HAVE MULTIPLE BANK ACCOUNTS?

## REASONS FOR HAVING MULTIPLE BANK ACCOUNTS

While managing one bank account might seem convenient, there are various situations where having multiple bank accounts can be beneficial:

1. **Budgeting:** Owning multiple accounts aids in budgeting by facilitating improved organization, allowing for the division of spending, savings, household expenses, and individual earnings for dependents.
2. **Tracking Savings Goals:** Tracking specific savings goals like retirement funds or stock market investments.
3. **Finances Separation:** For couples and partners who prefer to maintain separate financial responsibilities, separate bank accounts enable personalized spending and saving arrangements.
4. **Teaching Financial Responsibility:** Opening a joint account with a child can teach them about money management and sticking to a budget at an early age.

Regardless of your motives for having multiple bank accounts, it's essential to start with the basics and gradually add accounts that align with your financial situation.

### PROS AND CONS OF MULTIPLE BANK ACCOUNTS

**PROS:**

- Easy tracking of different types of transactions.
- Reduced dependency on one bank.
- Helps keeping a track of retirement, emergency savings, without the fear of spending.
- A separate account for home (domestic) purpose and salary account.
- Having different kids account can be helpful to raise money-wise kids.

**CONS:**

- Maintaining the average/minimum balance in each account
- In-efficient use of your funds
- Problems relating to the dormancy of accounts.
- Managing and monitoring all accounts.

**SUMMARY**

As you can see, having multiple bank accounts can pose lots of benefits as well as challenges to you. Hence, before opening another savings account, ensure that you assess your financial situation carefully.

"The secret of change is to focus all of your energy not on fighting the old but on building the new." - Socrates

**Disclaimer: This part is solely for educational purposes. The investments quoted here are not recommendatory.**

# BANK ACCOUNT INFO

## BANK NAME

IFSC CODE & BRANCH:

ACCOUNT NO.

ACCOUNT USERNAME:

CONTACT NO: EMAIL LINKED:

ADDRESS:

DEBIT CARD: CREDIT CARD:

ACCOUNT TYPE: SAVING ☐ INVESTMENT ☐ CURRENT ☐ OTHER ☐

NOMINEE

PURPOSE OF ACC:

## DEBIT CARD

CARD NO.

CARD HOLDER:

EXPIRY: (MM/YY)

CONTACT:

OTHER INFO:

## DEBIT CARD

CARD NO.

CARD HOLDER:

EXPIRY: (MM/YY)

CONTACT:

OTHER INFO:

CARD NO.

CARD HOLDER:

EXPIRY: (MM/YY)

CONTACT:

OTHER INFO:

CARD NO.

CARD HOLDER:

EXPIRY: (MM/YY)

CONTACT:

OTHER INFO:

"Wealth is not about having a lot of money; it's about having a lot of options." - Chris Rock

**Pro Tip : Write your CVV no in pencil Or skip that part since its risky**

# BANK ACCOUNT INFO

**BANK NAME**

IFSC CODE & BRANCH:

ACCOUNT NO.

ACCOUNT USERNAME:

CONTACT NO: EMAIL LINKED:

ADDRESS:

DEBIT CARD: CREDIT CARD:

ACCOUNT TYPE: SAVING ☐ INVESTMENT ☐ CURRENT ☐ OTHER ☐

NOMINEE

PURPOSE OF ACC:

**DEBIT CARD**

CARD NO.

CARD HOLDER:

EXPIRY: (MM/YY)

CONTACT:

OTHER INFO:

**DEBIT CARD**

CARD NO.

CARD HOLDER:

EXPIRY: (MM/YY)

CONTACT:

OTHER INFO:

CARD NO.

CARD HOLDER:

EXPIRY: (MM/YY)

CONTACT:

OTHER INFO:

CARD NO.

CARD HOLDER:

EXPIRY: (MM/YY)

CONTACT:

OTHER INFO:

"Don't tell me what you value, show me your budget, and I'll tell you what you value." – Joe Biden

**Pro Tip : Write your CVV no in pencil Or skip that part since its risky**

# BANK ACCOUNT INFO

**BANK NAME**

IFSC CODE & BRANCH:

ACCOUNT NO.

ACCOUNT USERNAME:

CONTACT NO: EMAIL LINKED:

ADDRESS:

DEBIT CARD: CREDIT CARD:

ACCOUNT TYPE: SAVING ☐ INVESTMENT ☐ CURRENT ☐ OTHER ☐

NOMINEE

PURPOSE OF ACC:

**DEBIT CARD**

CARD NO.

CARD HOLDER:

EXPIRY: (MM/YY)

CONTACT:

OTHER INFO:

**DEBIT CARD**

CARD NO.

CARD HOLDER:

EXPIRY: (MM/YY)

CONTACT:

OTHER INFO:

CARD NO.

CARD HOLDER:

EXPIRY: (MM/YY)

CONTACT:

OTHER INFO:

CARD NO.

CARD HOLDER:

EXPIRY: (MM/YY)

CONTACT:

OTHER INFO:

"Start saving and investing early in life. Time is your greatest asset." - Warren Buffett

**Pro Tip: Write your CVV no in pencil Or skip that part since its risky**

# BANK ACCOUNT INFO

**BANK NAME**

IFSC CODE & BRANCH:

ACCOUNT NO.

ACCOUNT USERNAME:

CONTACT NO: EMAIL LINKED:

ADDRESS:

DEBIT CARD: CREDIT CARD:

ACCOUNT TYPE: SAVING ☐ INVESTMENT ☐ CURRENT ☐ OTHER ☐

NOMINEE

PURPOSE OF ACC:

**DEBIT CARD**

CARD NO.

CARD HOLDER:

EXPIRY: (MM/YY)

CONTACT:

OTHER INFO:

**DEBIT CARD**

CARD NO.

CARD HOLDER:

EXPIRY: (MM/YY)

CONTACT:

OTHER INFO:

CARD NO.

CARD HOLDER:

EXPIRY: (MM/YY)

CONTACT:

OTHER INFO:

CARD NO.

CARD HOLDER:

EXPIRY: (MM/YY)

CONTACT:

OTHER INFO:

"Money is only a tool. It will take you wherever you wish, but it will not replace you as the driver."
- Ayn Rand

**Pro Tip: Write your CVV no in pencil Or skip that part since its risky**

# BANK ACCOUNT INFO

## BANK NAME

IFSC CODE & BRANCH:

ACCOUNT NO.

ACCOUNT USERNAME:

CONTACT NO: EMAIL LINKED:

ADDRESS:

DEBIT CARD: CREDIT CARD:

ACCOUNT TYPE: SAVING ☐ INVESTMENT ☐ CURRENT ☐ OTHER ☐

NOMINEE

PURPOSE OF ACC:

## DEBIT CARD

CARD NO.

CARD HOLDER:

EXPIRY: (MM/YY)

CONTACT:

OTHER INFO:

## DEBIT CARD

CARD NO.

CARD HOLDER:

EXPIRY: (MM/YY)

CONTACT:

OTHER INFO:

CARD NO.

CARD HOLDER:

EXPIRY: (MM/YY)

CONTACT:

OTHER INFO:

CARD NO.

CARD HOLDER:

EXPIRY: (MM/YY)

CONTACT:

OTHER INFO:

"A budget is telling your money where to go instead of wondering where it went." - Dave Ramsey

**Pro Tip : Write your CVV no in pencil Or skip that part since its risky**

# BANK ACCOUNT INFO

**BANK NAME**

IFSC CODE & BRANCH:

ACCOUNT NO.

ACCOUNT USERNAME:

CONTACT NO: EMAIL LINKED:

ADDRESS:

DEBIT CARD: CREDIT CARD:

ACCOUNT TYPE: SAVING ☐ INVESTMENT ☐ CURRENT ☐ OTHER ☐

NOMINEE

PURPOSE OF ACC:

**DEBIT CARD**

CARD NO.

CARD HOLDER:

EXPIRY: (MM/YY)

CONTACT:

OTHER INFO:

**DEBIT CARD**

CARD NO.

CARD HOLDER:

EXPIRY: (MM/YY)

CONTACT:

OTHER INFO:

CARD NO.

CARD HOLDER:

EXPIRY: (MM/YY)

CONTACT:

OTHER INFO:

CARD NO.

CARD HOLDER:

EXPIRY: (MM/YY)

CONTACT:

OTHER INFO:

"The more you learn, the more you earn." - Warren Buffett

**Pro Tip: Write your CVV no in pencil Or skip that part since its risky**

# BANK ACCOUNT INFO

## BANK NAME

IFSC CODE & BRANCH:

ACCOUNT NO.

ACCOUNT USERNAME:

CONTACT NO: EMAIL LINKED:

ADDRESS:

DEBIT CARD: CREDIT CARD:

ACCOUNT TYPE: SAVING ☐ INVESTMENT ☐ CURRENT ☐ OTHER ☐

NOMINEE

PURPOSE OF ACC:

## DEBIT CARD

CARD NO.

CARD HOLDER:

EXPIRY: (MM/YY)

CONTACT:

OTHER INFO:

## DEBIT CARD

CARD NO.

CARD HOLDER:

EXPIRY: (MM/YY)

CONTACT:

OTHER INFO:

CARD NO.

CARD HOLDER:

EXPIRY: (MM/YY)

CONTACT:

OTHER INFO:

CARD NO.

CARD HOLDER:

EXPIRY: (MM/YY)

CONTACT:

OTHER INFO:

"An investment in knowledge pays the best interest." - Benjamin Franklin

**Pro Tip : Write your CVV no in pencil Or skip that part since its risky**

# BANK ACCOUNT INFO

BANK NAME

IFSC CODE & BRANCH:

ACCOUNT NO.

ACCOUNT USERNAME:

CONTACT NO: EMAIL LINKED:

ADDRESS:

DEBIT CARD: CREDIT CARD:

ACCOUNT TYPE: SAVING ☐ INVESTMENT ☐ CURRENT ☐ OTHER ☐

NOMINEE

PURPOSE OF ACC:

## DEBIT CARD

CARD NO.

CARD HOLDER:

EXPIRY: (MM/YY)

CONTACT:

OTHER INFO:

## DEBIT CARD

CARD NO.

CARD HOLDER:

EXPIRY: (MM/YY)

CONTACT:

OTHER INFO:

CARD NO.

CARD HOLDER:

EXPIRY: (MM/YY)

CONTACT:

OTHER INFO:

CARD NO.

CARD HOLDER:

EXPIRY: (MM/YY)

CONTACT:

OTHER INFO:

"The only thing that overcomes hard luck is hard work." - Harry Golden

**Pro Tip : Write your CVV no in pencil Or skip that part since its risky**

# BANK ACCOUNT INFO

## BANK NAME

IFSC CODE & BRANCH:

ACCOUNT NO.

ACCOUNT USERNAME:

CONTACT NO: EMAIL LINKED:

ADDRESS:

DEBIT CARD: CREDIT CARD:

ACCOUNT TYPE: SAVING ☐ INVESTMENT ☐ CURRENT ☐ OTHER ☐

NOMINEE

PURPOSE OF ACC:

## DEBIT CARD

CARD NO.

CARD HOLDER:

EXPIRY: (MM/YY)

CONTACT:

OTHER INFO:

## DEBIT CARD

CARD NO.

CARD HOLDER:

EXPIRY: (MM/YY)

CONTACT:

OTHER INFO:

CARD NO.

CARD HOLDER:

EXPIRY: (MM/YY)

CONTACT:

OTHER INFO:

CARD NO.

CARD HOLDER:

EXPIRY: (MM/YY)

CONTACT:

OTHER INFO:

"We should remember that good fortune often happens when opportunity meets with preparation." - Thomas Edison

**Pro Tip: Write your CVV no in pencil Or skip that part since its risky**

# BANK ACCOUNT INFO

## BANK NAME

IFSC CODE & BRANCH:

ACCOUNT NO.

ACCOUNT USERNAME:

CONTACT NO: EMAIL LINKED:

ADDRESS:

DEBIT CARD: CREDIT CARD:

ACCOUNT TYPE: SAVING ☐ INVESTMENT ☐ CURRENT ☐ OTHER ☐

NOMINEE

PURPOSE OF ACC:

## DEBIT CARD

CARD NO.

CARD HOLDER:

EXPIRY: (MM/YY)

CONTACT:

OTHER INFO:

## DEBIT CARD

CARD NO.

CARD HOLDER:

EXPIRY: (MM/YY)

CONTACT:

OTHER INFO:

CARD NO.

CARD HOLDER:

EXPIRY: (MM/YY)

CONTACT:

OTHER INFO:

CARD NO.

CARD HOLDER:

EXPIRY: (MM/YY)

CONTACT:

OTHER INFO:

"A penny saved is a penny earned."- Anonymous

**Pro Tip: Write your CVV no in pencil Or skip that part since its risky**

# BANK ACCOUNT INFO

**BANK NAME**

IFSC CODE & BRANCH:

ACCOUNT NO.

ACCOUNT USERNAME:

CONTACT NO: EMAIL LINKED:

ADDRESS:

DEBIT CARD: CREDIT CARD:

ACCOUNT TYPE: SAVING ☐ INVESTMENT ☐ CURRENT ☐ OTHER ☐

NOMINEE

PURPOSE OF ACC:

**DEBIT CARD**

CARD NO.

CARD HOLDER:

EXPIRY: (MM/YY)

CONTACT:

OTHER INFO:

**DEBIT CARD**

CARD NO.

CARD HOLDER:

EXPIRY: (MM/YY)

CONTACT:

OTHER INFO:

CARD NO.

CARD HOLDER:

EXPIRY: (MM/YY)

CONTACT:

OTHER INFO:

CARD NO.

CARD HOLDER:

EXPIRY: (MM/YY)

CONTACT:

OTHER INFO:

"When money realizes that it is in good hands, it wants to stay and multiply in those hands." - Idowu Koyenikan

**Pro Tip : Write your CVV no in pencil Or skip that part since its risky**

# UPI ACCOUNT TRACKER

| No. | UPI ACCOUNT | UPI ID | LINKED BANK A/C | REGISTERED NO. |
|---|---|---|---|---|
| 1 | Paytm | | | |
| 2 | Google Pay | | | |
| 3 | | | | |
| 4 | | | | |
| 5 | | | | |
| 6 | | | | |
| 7 | | | | |
| 8 | | | | |
| 9 | | | | |
| 10 | | | | |
| 11 | | | | |
| 12 | | | | |
| 13 | | | | |
| 14 | | | | |
| 15 | | | | |
| 16 | | | | |
| 17 | | | | |
| 18 | | | | |
| 19 | | | | |
| 20 | | | | |

*Notes*

"Money doesn't talk, it swears."- Bob Dylan

**Pro Tip: Keep a track of your UPI monthly payments and you'll be surprised!**

# DEBIT CARD TRACKER

| No. | CARD HOLDER NAME | BANK NAME | CARD NUMBER | REGISTERED NO | VALIDITY |
|---|---|---|---|---|---|
| 1 | | | | | |
| 2 | | | | | |
| 3 | | | | | |
| 4 | | | | | |
| 5 | | | | | |
| 6 | | | | | |
| 7 | | | | | |
| 8 | | | | | |
| 9 | | | | | |
| 10 | | | | | |
| 11 | | | | | |
| 12 | | | | | |
| 13 | | | | | |
| 14 | | | | | |
| 15 | | | | | |
| 16 | | | | | |
| 17 | | | | | |
| 18 | | | | | |
| 19 | | | | | |
| 20 | | | | | |

*Notes* ..............................................................................................

.............................................................................................................

.............................................................................................................

.............................................................................................................

.............................................................................................................

Debit Cards provide convenience of cash withdrawals or card payments in-person or online

# CREDIT CARDS TRACKER

| No. | CARD HOLDER NAME | CARD NUMBER | LINKED A/C | REGISTERED NO. |
|---|---|---|---|---|
| 1 | | | | |
| 2 | | | | |
| 3 | | | | |
| 4 | | | | |
| 5 | | | | |
| 6 | | | | |
| 7 | | | | |
| 8 | | | | |
| 9 | | | | |
| 10 | | | | |
| 11 | | | | |
| 12 | | | | |
| 13 | | | | |
| 14 | | | | |
| 15 | | | | |
| 16 | | | | |
| 17 | | | | |
| 18 | | | | |
| 19 | | | | |
| 20 | | | | |
| 21 | | | | |
| 22 | | | | |
| 23 | | | | |
| 24 | | | | |
| 25 | | | | |

"Credit card spending is about borrowing from future joy to make the present happy"- Anonymous

| CARD NAME | CREDIT LIMIT | BC DATE | VALIDITY | REMARKS |
| --- | --- | --- | --- | --- |
| | | | | |
| | | | | |
| | | | | |
| | | | | |
| | | | | |
| | | | | |
| | | | | |
| | | | | |
| | | | | |
| | | | | |
| | | | | |
| | | | | |
| | | | | |
| | | | | |
| | | | | |
| | | | | |
| | | | | |
| | | | | |
| | | | | |
| | | | | |
| | | | | |
| | | | | |
| | | | | |
| | | | | |
| | | | | |

"Truth is like a debit card, Pay first enjoy later. Lie is like a credit card, enjoy first pay later."

ATM
ASSETS
$1,223,400

# ASSET CLASSES

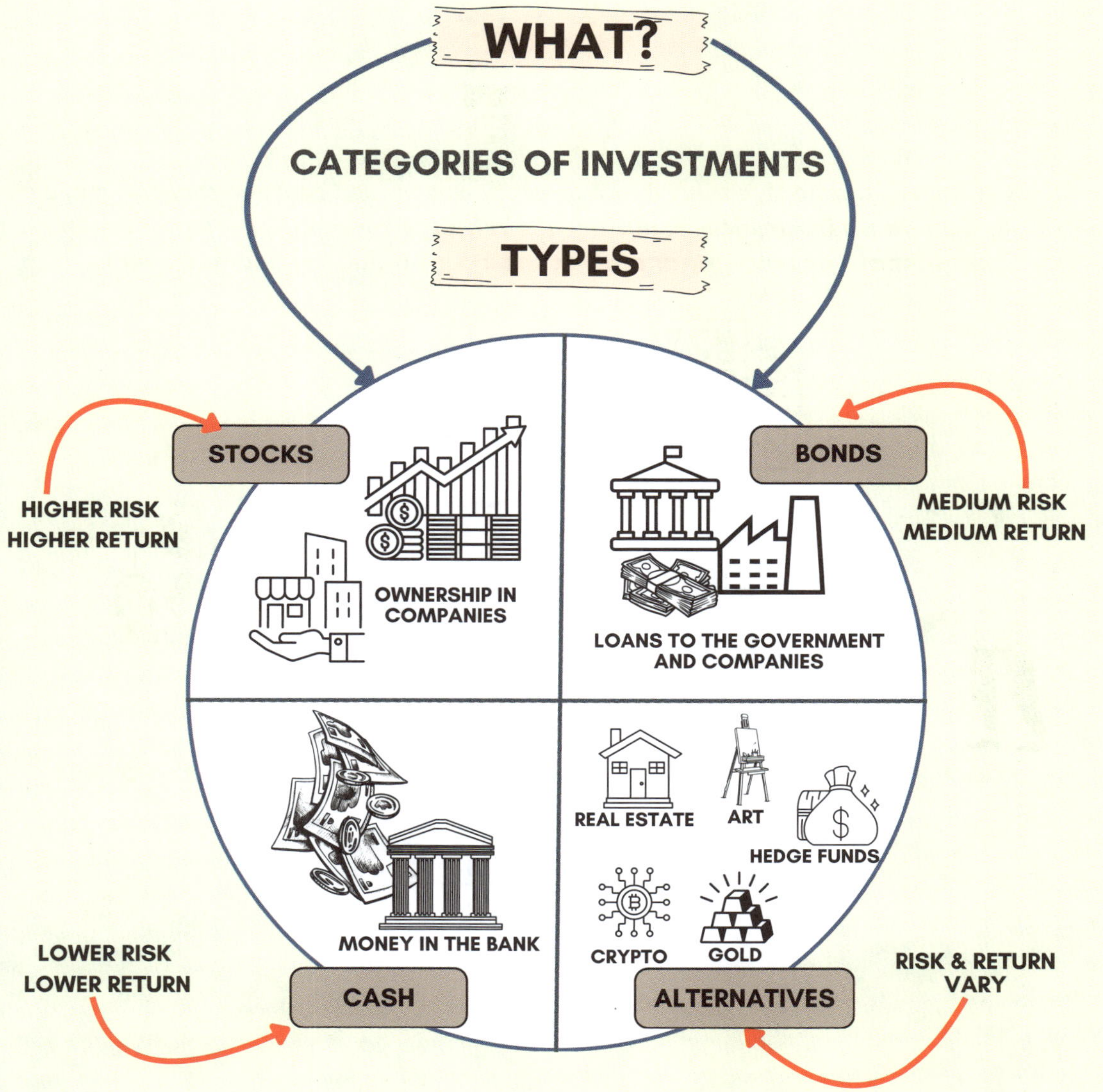


**Page Inspiration: @Napkin Finance**

Disclaimer: This page designed by Muneem Khaata, is purely for educational purposes only. And not a financial advisory.

# INSURANCE

Insurance is a financial arrangement that provides ***protection*** against the ***risk*** of financial loss.

In an insurance contract, an individual or entity, known as ***the policyholder***, ***pays*** a premium ***to an insurance company*** in ***exchange*** for the insurer's promise to ***compensate or cover financial losses*** incurred due to specified events.

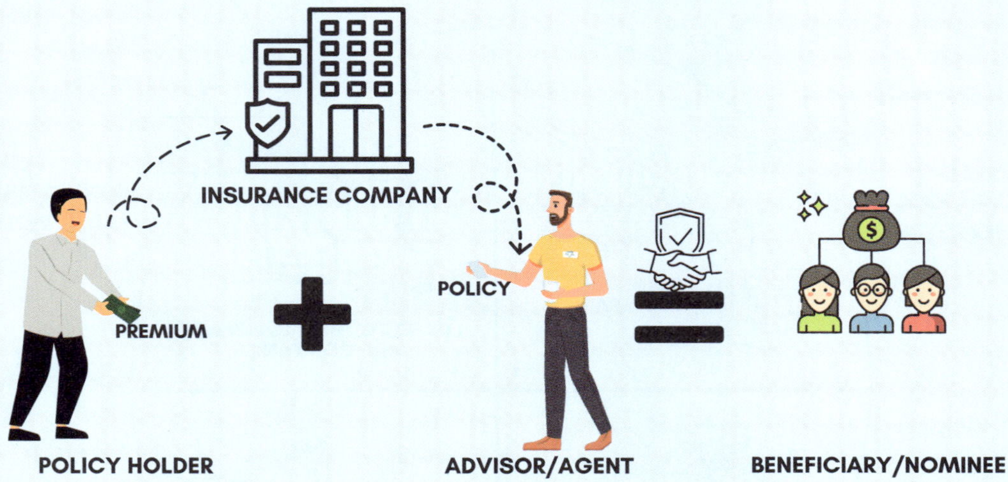


## INSURANCE SYSTEM

### KEY COMPONENTS OF INSURANCE

**Premium:** The amount paid by the policyholder to the insurance company at regular intervals

**Policy:** The insurance contract that outlines the terms and conditions of coverage

**Insurer:** The insurance company that assumes the financial risk and obligation to compensate the policyholder

**Policyholder:** The specific risks or perils for which the insurance policy provides protection.

**Coverage:** The specific risks or perils for which the insurance policy provides protection.

**Beneficiary:** The person or entity designated by the policyholder to receive the benefits or compensation in case of the policyholder's death (in the case of life insurance) or under other specified circumstances.

# BENEFITS OF INSURANCE & ITS TYPES

## BENEFITS

UNFORESEEN EXPENSES

DEATH

SECURES FAMILY

TAX REDUCTION

- Helps achieve Long Term Goals
- To take care of your loved ones
- Creates a source of saving.
- Supplements Your Retirement Goals
- Contributes to overall economic stability
- Takes care of unexpected expenses

## SOME TYPES OF INSURANCE POLICIES

LIFE INSURANCE

DISABILITY INSURANCE

HEALTH INSURANCE

HOME/PROPERTY INSURANCE

VEHICLE INSURANCE

TRAVEL INSURANCE

ENDOWMENT POLICY
Example :ULIP

BUSINESS INSURANCE

TERM INSURANCE

### THINGS TO CONSIDER BEFORE BUYING INSURANCE

- Choose the right insurance provider.
- Choose adequate coverage.
- Add suitable rider, if needed.
- Know the Claiming Process of the provider.
- Provide accurate and true information.
- It is better to take a separate health insurance for Sr. Citizen of the family member as the premium is high compared to adults.
- Read all the offer documents before investing.

# LIFE/ TERM INSURANCE

**POLICY HOLDER NAME:**

NAME OF POLICY: ____________________
NATURE OF POLICY: ____________________
INSURANCE COMPANY: ____________________
WEBSITE: ____________________ CONTACT COMPANY: ____________________
BRANCH CODE: ____________________ AGENT/INTERMEDIARY NAME: ____________________
CONTACT AGENT/INTERMEDIARY: ____________________ GSTIN/UIN: ____________________

POLICY NO: ____________________
POLICY HOLDER CONTACT: ____________________ EMAIL: ____________________
REGISTERED ADDRESS: ____________________
SUM INSURED: ____________________ PREMIUM AMOUNT: ____________________
ISSUED DATE: ____________________ PREMIUM DUE DATE: ____________________
PREMIUM PAYING YEARS: ____________________ FREQUENCY: ____________________

NOMINEE NAME: ____________________ RELATIONSHIP WITH NOMINEE: ____________________
SHARE: ____________________ BENEFITS: ____________________

ADDTL INFO: ____________________
____________________

**POLICY HOLDER NAME:**

NAME OF POLICY: ____________________
NATURE OF POLICY: ____________________
INSURANCE COMPANY: ____________________
WEBSITE: ____________________ CONTACT COMPANY: ____________________
BRANCH CODE: ____________________ AGENT/INTERMEDIARY NAME: ____________________
CONTACT AGENT/INTERMEDIARY: ____________________ GSTIN/UIN: ____________________

POLICY NO: ____________________
POLICY HOLDER CONTACT: ____________________ EMAIL: ____________________
REGISTERED ADDRESS: ____________________
SUM INSURED: ____________________ PREMIUM AMOUNT: ____________________
ISSUED DATE: ____________________ PREMIUM DUE DATE: ____________________
PREMIUM PAYING YEARS: ____________________ FREQUENCY: ____________________

NOMINEE NAME: ____________________ RELATIONSHIP WITH NOMINEE: ____________________
SHARE: ____________________ BENEFITS: ____________________

ADDTL INFO: ____________________
____________________

"The basic purpose of life insurance is to create cash... Nothing more or nothing less... Everything else confuses and complicates." - Anonymous

# LIFE/ TERM INSURANCE

**POLICY HOLDER NAME:**

NAME OF POLICY: ____________________

NATURE OF POLICY: ____________________

INSURANCE COMPANY: ____________________

WEBSITE: ____________________ CONTACT COMPANY: ____________________

BRANCH CODE: ____________________ AGENT/INTERMEDIARY NAME: ____________________

CONTACT AGENT/INTERMEDIARY: ____________________ GSTIN/UIN: ____________________

POLICY NO: ____________________

POLICY HOLDER CONTACT: ____________________ EMAIL: ____________________

REGISTERED ADDRESS: ____________________

SUM INSURED: ____________________ PREMIUM AMOUNT: ____________________

ISSUED DATE: ____________________ PREMIUM DUE DATE: ____________________

PREMIUM PAYING YEARS: ____________________ FREQUENCY: ____________________

NOMINEE NAME: ____________________ RELATIONSHIP WITH NOMINEE: ____________________

SHARE: ____________________ BENEFITS: ____________________

ADDTL INFO: ____________________

____________________

**POLICY HOLDER NAME:**

NAME OF POLICY: ____________________

NATURE OF POLICY: ____________________

INSURANCE COMPANY: ____________________

WEBSITE: ____________________ CONTACT COMPANY: ____________________

BRANCH CODE: ____________________ AGENT/INTERMEDIARY NAME: ____________________

CONTACT AGENT/INTERMEDIARY: ____________________ GSTIN/UIN: ____________________

POLICY NO: ____________________

POLICY HOLDER CONTACT: ____________________ EMAIL: ____________________

REGISTERED ADDRESS: ____________________

SUM INSURED: ____________________ PREMIUM AMOUNT: ____________________

ISSUED DATE: ____________________ PREMIUM DUE DATE: ____________________

PREMIUM PAYING YEARS: ____________________ FREQUENCY: ____________________

NOMINEE NAME: ____________________ RELATIONSHIP WITH NOMINEE: ____________________

SHARE: ____________________ BENEFITS: ____________________

ADDTL INFO: ____________________

____________________

"You don't buy life insurance because you are going to die, but because those you love are going to live."
- Anonymous

# HEALTH INSURANCE

**POLICY HOLDER NAME:**

NAME OF POLICY: ____________________
NATURE OF POLICY: ____________________
INSURANCE COMPANY: ____________________
WEBSITE: ____________________ CONTACT COMPANY: ____________________
BRANCH CODE: ____________________ AGENT/INTERMEDIARY NAME : ____________________
CONTACT AGENT/INTERMEDIARY: ____________________ GSTIN/UIN: ____________________

POLICY NO: ____________________
POLICY HOLDER CONTACT: ____________________ EMAIL: ____________________
REGISTERED ADDRESS: ____________________
SUM INSURED: ____________________ PREMIUM AMOUNT: ____________________
ISSUED DATE: ____________________ PREMIUM DUE DATE: ____________________
FIRST POLICY INCEPTION DATE: ____________________ PERIOD OF INSURANCE: ____________________

INSURED PERSONS: __________ MEMBER 1 : ____________________ MEMBER 2 : ____________________
MEMBER 3 : ____________________ MEMBER 4 : ____________________
SHARE: ____________________ BENEFITS: ____________________

ADDTL INFO: ____________________
____________________

**POLICY HOLDER NAME:**

NAME OF POLICY: ____________________
NATURE OF POLICY: ____________________
INSURANCE COMPANY: ____________________
WEBSITE: ____________________ CONTACT COMPANY: ____________________
BRANCH CODE: ____________________ AGENT/INTERMEDIARY NAME : ____________________
CONTACT AGENT/INTERMEDIARY: ____________________ GSTIN/UIN: ____________________

POLICY NO: ____________________
POLICY HOLDER CONTACT: ____________________ EMAIL: ____________________
REGISTERED ADDRESS: ____________________
SUM INSURED: ____________________ PREMIUM AMOUNT: ____________________
ISSUED DATE: ____________________ PREMIUM DUE DATE: ____________________
FIRST POLICY INCEPTION DATE: ____________________ PERIOD OF INSURANCE: ____________________

INSURED PERSONS: __________ MEMBER 1 : ____________________ MEMBER 2 : ____________________
MEMBER 3 : ____________________ MEMBER 4 : ____________________
SHARE: ____________________ BENEFITS: ____________________

ADDTL INFO: ____________________
____________________

"The greatest wealth is to live content with little." - Plato

# HEALTH INSURANCE

**POLICY HOLDER NAME:**

NAME OF POLICY: ______________________

NATURE OF POLICY: ______________________

INSURANCE COMPANY: ______________________

WEBSITE: ______________ CONTACT COMPANY: ______________

BRANCH CODE: ______________ AGENT/INTERMEDIARY NAME : ______________

CONTACT AGENT/INTERMEDIARY: ______________ GSTIN/UIN: ______________

POLICY NO: ______________________

POLICY HOLDER CONTACT: ______________ EMAIL: ______________

REGISTERED ADDRESS: ______________________

SUM INSURED: ______________ PREMIUM AMOUNT: ______________

ISSUED DATE: ______________ PREMIUM DUE DATE: ______________

FIRST POLICY INCEPTION DATE: ______________ PERIOD OF INSURANCE: ______________

INSURED PERSONS: __________ MEMBER 1 : ______________ MEMBER 2 : ______________

MEMBER 3 : ______________ MEMBER 4 : ______________

SHARE: ______________ BENEFITS: ______________

ADDITIONAL INFO: ______________________

______________________

**POLICY HOLDER NAME:**

NAME OF POLICY: ______________________

NATURE OF POLICY: ______________________

INSURANCE COMPANY: ______________________

WEBSITE: ______________ CONTACT COMPANY: ______________

BRANCH CODE: ______________ AGENT/INTERMEDIARY NAME : ______________

CONTACT AGENT/INTERMEDIARY: ______________ GSTIN/UIN: ______________

POLICY NO: ______________________

POLICY HOLDER CONTACT: ______________ EMAIL: ______________

REGISTERED ADDRESS: ______________________

SUM INSURED: ______________ PREMIUM AMOUNT: ______________

ISSUED DATE: ______________ PREMIUM DUE DATE: ______________

FIRST POLICY INCEPTION DATE: ______________ PERIOD OF INSURANCE: ______________

INSURED PERSONS: __________ MEMBER 1 : ______________ MEMBER 2 : ______________

MEMBER 3 : ______________ MEMBER 4 : ______________

SHARE: ______________ BENEFITS: ______________

ADDITIONAL INFO: ______________________

______________________

"He who has health has hope and he who has hope has everything."– Arabian Proverb

# POLICIES

**POLICY HOLDER NAME:**

NAME OF POLICY: ____________________

NATURE OF POLICY: ____________________

INSURANCE COMPANY: ____________________

WEBSITE: ____________________ CONTACT COMPANY: ____________________

BRANCH CODE: ____________________ AGENT/INTERMEDIARY NAME : ____________________

CONTACT AGENT/INTERMEDIARY: ____________________ GSTIN/UIN: ____________________

POLICY NO: ____________________

POLICY HOLDER CONTACT: ____________________ EMAIL: ____________________

REGISTERED ADDRESS: ____________________

SUM INSURED: ____________________ PREMIUM AMOUNT: ____________________

ISSUED DATE: ____________________ PREMIUM DUE DATE: ____________________

FIRST POLICY INCEPTION DATE: ____________________ PERIOD OF INSURANCE: ____________________

NOMINEE NAME: ____________________ RELATIONSHIP WITH NOMINEE: ____________________

SHARE: ____________________ BENEFITS: ____________________

ADDTL INFO: ____________________

____________________

**POLICY HOLDER NAME:**

NAME OF POLICY: ____________________

NATURE OF POLICY: ____________________

INSURANCE COMPANY: ____________________

WEBSITE: ____________________ CONTACT COMPANY: ____________________

BRANCH CODE: ____________________ AGENT/INTERMEDIARY NAME : ____________________

CONTACT AGENT/INTERMEDIARY: ____________________ GSTIN/UIN: ____________________

POLICY NO: ____________________

POLICY HOLDER CONTACT: ____________________ EMAIL: ____________________

REGISTERED ADDRESS: ____________________

SUM INSURED: ____________________ PREMIUM AMOUNT: ____________________

ISSUED DATE: ____________________ PREMIUM DUE DATE: ____________________

FIRST POLICY INCEPTION DATE: ____________________ PERIOD OF INSURANCE: ____________________

NOMINEE NAME: ____________________ RELATIONSHIP WITH NOMINEE: ____________________

SHARE: ____________________ BENEFITS: ____________________

ADDTL INFO: ____________________

____________________

"It's not the man who has too little, but the man who craves more, that is poor." - Seneca

# POLICIES

**POLICY HOLDER NAME:**

NAME OF POLICY: ______

NATURE OF POLICY: ______

INSURANCE COMPANY: ______

WEBSITE: ______ CONTACT COMPANY: ______

BRANCH CODE: ______ AGENT/INTERMEDIARY NAME : ______

CONTACT AGENT/INTERMEDIARY: ______ GSTIN/UIN: ______

POLICY NO: ______

POLICY HOLDER CONTACT: ______ EMAIL: ______

REGISTERED ADDRESS: ______

SUM INSURED: ______ PREMIUM AMOUNT: ______

ISSUED DATE: ______ PREMIUM DUE DATE: ______

FIRST POLICY INCEPTION DATE: ______ PERIOD OF INSURANCE: ______

NOMINEE NAME: ______ RELATIONSHIP WITH NOMINEE: ______

SHARE: ______ BENEFITS: ______

ADDTL INFO: ______

______

**POLICY HOLDER NAME:**

NAME OF POLICY: ______

NATURE OF POLICY: ______

INSURANCE COMPANY: ______

WEBSITE: ______ CONTACT COMPANY: ______

BRANCH CODE: ______ AGENT/INTERMEDIARY NAME : ______

CONTACT AGENT/INTERMEDIARY: ______ GSTIN/UIN: ______

POLICY NO: ______

POLICY HOLDER CONTACT: ______ EMAIL: ______

REGISTERED ADDRESS: ______

SUM INSURED: ______ PREMIUM AMOUNT: ______

ISSUED DATE: ______ PREMIUM DUE DATE: ______

FIRST POLICY INCEPTION DATE: ______ PERIOD OF INSURANCE: ______

NOMINEE NAME: ______ RELATIONSHIP WITH NOMINEE: ______

SHARE: ______ BENEFITS: ______

ADDTL INFO: ______

______

"Always try to rub up against money, for if you rub up against money long enough, some of it may rub off on you." - Damon Runyon

# POLICIES

**POLICY HOLDER NAME:**

NAME OF POLICY: ____________________

NATURE OF POLICY: ____________________

INSURANCE COMPANY: ____________________

WEBSITE: ____________________ CONTACT COMPANY: ____________________

BRANCH CODE: ____________________ AGENT/INTERMEDIARY NAME : ____________________

CONTACT AGENT/INTERMEDIARY: ____________________ GSTIN/UIN: ____________________

POLICY NO: ____________________

POLICY HOLDER CONTACT: ____________________ EMAIL: ____________________

REGISTERED ADDRESS: ____________________

SUM INSURED: ____________________ PREMIUM AMOUNT: ____________________

ISSUED DATE: ____________________ PREMIUM DUE DATE: ____________________

FIRST POLICY INCEPTION DATE: ____________________ PERIOD OF INSURANCE: ____________________

NOMINEE NAME: ____________________ RELATIONSHIP WITH NOMINEE: ____________________

SHARE: ____________________ BENEFITS: ____________________

ADDTL INFO: ____________________

____________________

**POLICY HOLDER NAME:**

NAME OF POLICY: ____________________

NATURE OF POLICY: ____________________

INSURANCE COMPANY: ____________________

WEBSITE: ____________________ CONTACT COMPANY: ____________________

BRANCH CODE: ____________________ AGENT/INTERMEDIARY NAME : ____________________

CONTACT AGENT/INTERMEDIARY: ____________________ GSTIN/UIN: ____________________

POLICY NO: ____________________

POLICY HOLDER CONTACT: ____________________ EMAIL: ____________________

REGISTERED ADDRESS: ____________________

SUM INSURED: ____________________ PREMIUM AMOUNT: ____________________

ISSUED DATE: ____________________ PREMIUM DUE DATE: ____________________

FIRST POLICY INCEPTION DATE: ____________________ PERIOD OF INSURANCE: ____________________

NOMINEE NAME: ____________________ RELATIONSHIP WITH NOMINEE: ____________________

SHARE: ____________________ BENEFITS: ____________________

ADDTL INFO: ____________________

____________________

"Making money isn't hard in itself. What's hard is to earn it doing something worth devoting one's life to."

- Carlos Ruiz Zafón

# POLICIES

**POLICY HOLDER NAME:**

NAME OF POLICY: ____________________

NATURE OF POLICY: ____________________

INSURANCE COMPANY: ____________________

WEBSITE: ____________ CONTACT COMPANY: ____________

BRANCH CODE: ____________ AGENT/INTERMEDIARY NAME : ____________

CONTACT AGENT/INTERMEDIARY: ____________ GSTIN/UIN: ____________

POLICY NO: ____________________

POLICY HOLDER CONTACT: ____________ EMAIL: ____________

REGISTERED ADDRESS: ____________________

SUM INSURED: ____________ PREMIUM AMOUNT: ____________

ISSUED DATE: ____________ PREMIUM DUE DATE: ____________

FIRST POLICY INCEPTION DATE: ____________ PERIOD OF INSURANCE: ____________

NOMINEE NAME: ____________ RELATIONSHIP WITH NOMINEE: ____________

SHARE: ____________ BENEFITS: ____________

ADDTL INFO: ____________________

____________________

**POLICY HOLDER NAME:**

NAME OF POLICY: ____________________

NATURE OF POLICY: ____________________

INSURANCE COMPANY: ____________________

WEBSITE: ____________ CONTACT COMPANY: ____________

BRANCH CODE: ____________ AGENT/INTERMEDIARY NAME : ____________

CONTACT AGENT/INTERMEDIARY: ____________ GSTIN/UIN: ____________

POLICY NO: ____________________

POLICY HOLDER CONTACT: ____________ EMAIL: ____________

REGISTERED ADDRESS: ____________________

SUM INSURED: ____________ PREMIUM AMOUNT: ____________

ISSUED DATE: ____________ PREMIUM DUE DATE: ____________

FIRST POLICY INCEPTION DATE: ____________ PERIOD OF INSURANCE: ____________

NOMINEE NAME: ____________ RELATIONSHIP WITH NOMINEE: ____________

SHARE: ____________ BENEFITS: ____________

ADDTL INFO: ____________________

____________________

"Too many people spend money they haven't earned, to buy things they don't want, to impress people that they don't like." - recorded by Robert Quillen

# POLICIES

**POLICY HOLDER NAME:**

NAME OF POLICY: ______________________________
NATURE OF POLICY: ______________________________
INSURANCE COMPANY: ______________________________
WEBSITE: ______________ CONTACT COMPANY: ______________
BRANCH CODE: ______________ AGENT/INTERMEDIARY NAME : ______________
CONTACT AGENT/INTERMEDIARY: ______________ GSTIN/UIN: ______________

POLICY NO: ______________________________
POLICY HOLDER CONTACT: ______________ EMAIL: ______________
REGISTERED ADDRESS: ______________________________
SUM INSURED: ______________ PREMIUM AMOUNT: ______________
ISSUED DATE: ______________ PREMIUM DUE DATE: ______________
FIRST POLICY INCEPTION DATE: ______________ PERIOD OF INSURANCE: ______________

NOMINEE NAME: ______________ RELATIONSHIP WITH NOMINEE: ______________
SHARE: ______________ BENEFITS: ______________

ADDTL INFO: ______________________________
______________________________

**POLICY HOLDER NAME:**

NAME OF POLICY: ______________________________
NATURE OF POLICY: ______________________________
INSURANCE COMPANY: ______________________________
WEBSITE: ______________ CONTACT COMPANY: ______________
BRANCH CODE: ______________ AGENT/INTERMEDIARY NAME : ______________
CONTACT AGENT/INTERMEDIARY: ______________ GSTIN/UIN: ______________

POLICY NO: ______________________________
POLICY HOLDER CONTACT: ______________ EMAIL: ______________
REGISTERED ADDRESS: ______________________________
SUM INSURED: ______________ PREMIUM AMOUNT: ______________
ISSUED DATE: ______________ PREMIUM DUE DATE: ______________
FIRST POLICY INCEPTION DATE: ______________ PERIOD OF INSURANCE: ______________

NOMINEE NAME: ______________ RELATIONSHIP WITH NOMINEE: ______________
SHARE: ______________ BENEFITS: ______________

ADDTL INFO: ______________________________
______________________________

"If wealth was the inevitable result of hard work and enterprise, every woman in Africa would be a millionaire."
- George Monbiot

# POLICIES

**POLICY HOLDER NAME:**

NAME OF POLICY: ____________________

NATURE OF POLICY: ____________________

INSURANCE COMPANY: ____________________

WEBSITE: ____________________ CONTACT COMPANY: ____________________

BRANCH CODE: ____________________ AGENT/INTERMEDIARY NAME : ____________________

CONTACT AGENT/INTERMEDIARY: ____________________ GSTIN/UIN: ____________________

POLICY NO: ____________________

POLICY HOLDER CONTACT: ____________________ EMAIL: ____________________

REGISTERED ADDRESS: ____________________

SUM INSURED: ____________________ PREMIUM AMOUNT: ____________________

ISSUED DATE: ____________________ PREMIUM DUE DATE: ____________________

FIRST POLICY INCEPTION DATE: ____________________ PERIOD OF INSURANCE: ____________________

NOMINEE NAME: ____________________ RELATIONSHIP WITH NOMINEE: ____________________

SHARE: ____________________ BENEFITS: ____________________

ADDTL INFO: ____________________

____________________

**POLICY HOLDER NAME:**

NAME OF POLICY: ____________________

NATURE OF POLICY: ____________________

INSURANCE COMPANY: ____________________

WEBSITE: ____________________ CONTACT COMPANY: ____________________

BRANCH CODE: ____________________ AGENT/INTERMEDIARY NAME : ____________________

CONTACT AGENT/INTERMEDIARY: ____________________ GSTIN/UIN: ____________________

POLICY NO: ____________________

POLICY HOLDER CONTACT: ____________________ EMAIL: ____________________

REGISTERED ADDRESS: ____________________

SUM INSURED: ____________________ PREMIUM AMOUNT: ____________________

ISSUED DATE: ____________________ PREMIUM DUE DATE: ____________________

FIRST POLICY INCEPTION DATE: ____________________ PERIOD OF INSURANCE: ____________________

NOMINEE NAME: ____________________ RELATIONSHIP WITH NOMINEE: ____________________

SHARE: ____________________ BENEFITS: ____________________

ADDTL INFO: ____________________

____________________

"Always try to rub up against money, for if you rub up against money long enough, some of it may rub off on you." - Damon Runyon

# VEHICLE INSURANCE TRACKER

| No. | VEHICLE NO | START DATE | END DATE | INSURANCE COMPANY | PREMIUM |
|---|---|---|---|---|---|
| 1 | | | | | |
| 2 | | | | | |
| 3 | | | | | |
| 4 | | | | | |
| 5 | | | | | |
| 6 | | | | | |
| 7 | | | | | |
| 8 | | | | | |
| 9 | | | | | |
| 10 | | | | | |
| 11 | | | | | |
| 12 | | | | | |
| 13 | | | | | |
| 14 | | | | | |
| 15 | | | | | |
| 16 | | | | | |
| 17 | | | | | |
| 18 | | | | | |
| 19 | | | | | |
| 20 | | | | | |
| 21 | | | | | |
| 22 | | | | | |
| 23 | | | | | |
| 24 | | | | | |
| 25 | | | | | |

"A journey of a thousand miles must begin with a single step." - Lao Tzu

# VEHICLE INSURANCE TRACKER

| INSURANCE COVER | POLICY NUMBER | REG. EMAIL | REG. NO. |
|---|---|---|---|
| | | | |
| | | | |
| | | | |
| | | | |
| | | | |
| | | | |
| | | | |
| | | | |
| | | | |
| | | | |
| | | | |
| | | | |
| | | | |
| | | | |
| | | | |
| | | | |
| | | | |
| | | | |
| | | | |
| | | | |
| | | | |
| | | | |
| | | | |
| | | | |
| | | | |

"Money can always be traced. It leaves a trail of slime behind it wherever it goes." - Michael Swanwick

# INSURANCE PREMIUM TRACKER

| No. | TYPE OF POLICY | POLICY NAME | HOLDER NAME | REG. NO | PREMIUM |
|---|---|---|---|---|---|
| 1 | Term | | | | |
| 2 | Health | | | | |
| 3 | | | | | |
| 4 | | | | | |
| 5 | | | | | |
| 6 | | | | | |
| 7 | | | | | |
| 8 | | | | | |
| 9 | | | | | |
| 10 | | | | | |
| 11 | | | | | |
| 12 | | | | | |
| 13 | | | | | |
| 14 | | | | | |
| 15 | | | | | |
| 16 | | | | | |
| 17 | | | | | |
| 18 | | | | | |
| 19 | | | | | |
| 20 | | | | | |
| 21 | | | | | |
| 22 | | | | | |
| 23 | | | | | |
| 24 | | | | | |
| 25 | | | | | |

"It's better to look ahead and prepare than to look back and regret." - Jackie Joyner-Kersee

# INSURANCE PREMIUM TRACKER

| POLICY NO. | ₹ INSURED | DUE DATE | PAID ON | MATURITY | REMARKS |
|---|---|---|---|---|---|
| | | | | | |
| | | | | | |
| | | | | | |
| | | | | | |
| | | | | | |
| | | | | | |
| | | | | | |
| | | | | | |
| | | | | | |
| | | | | | |
| | | | | | |
| | | | | | |
| | | | | | |
| | | | | | |
| | | | | | |
| | | | | | |
| | | | | | |
| | | | | | |
| | | | | | |
| | | | | | |
| | | | | | |
| | | | | | |
| | | | | | |
| | | | | | |
| | | | | | |

"A good plan, violently executed now, is better than a perfect plan next week." - George Patton

# MEMBERSHIP TRACKER

| No. | TYPE | NAME MEMBERSHIP | MEMBERSHIP NUMBER |
|---|---|---|---|
| 1 | | | |
| 2 | | | |
| 3 | | | |
| 4 | | | |
| 5 | | | |
| 6 | | | |
| 7 | | | |
| 8 | | | |
| 9 | | | |
| 10 | | | |
| 11 | | | |
| 12 | | | |
| 13 | | | |
| 14 | | | |
| 15 | | | |
| 16 | | | |
| 17 | | | |
| 18 | | | |
| 19 | | | |
| 20 | | | |
| 21 | | | |
| 22 | | | |
| 23 | | | |
| 24 | | | |
| 25 | | | |

"It's easy to say you don't care about money when you have plenty of it."- Ransom Riggs

| MEMBER NAME | PREMIUM AMOUNT | START DATE | RENEWAL | VALID TILL | NOMINEE |
|---|---|---|---|---|---|
| | | | | | |
| | | | | | |
| | | | | | |
| | | | | | |
| | | | | | |
| | | | | | |
| | | | | | |
| | | | | | |
| | | | | | |
| | | | | | |
| | | | | | |
| | | | | | |
| | | | | | |
| | | | | | |
| | | | | | |
| | | | | | |
| | | | | | |
| | | | | | |
| | | | | | |
| | | | | | |
| | | | | | |
| | | | | | |
| | | | | | |
| | | | | | |
| | | | | | |

**This page includes Airlines Membership, Hotels, Timeshare memberships etc. which may or may not be transferred to the family members.**

“A good plan, violently executed now, is better than a perfect plan next week.” - George Patton

# TYPE OF INVESTMENTS

STOCK MARKET

BOND & DEBENTURES

DEPOSITS

MUTUAL FUNDS

PPF(PUBLIC PROVIDENT FUND)

NATIONAL PENSION SCHEME NPS

SENIOR CITIZEN
SAVING SCHEME

GOLD

CRYPTOCURRENCY

GOVERNMENT SCHEMES

PROPERTY/REAL ESTATE

COMMODITIES

IPO (INTIAL PUBLIC OFFERING)

# TIME HORIZON IN INVESTMENT

An investment time horizon is the period an investment is held, categorized as short-term, medium-term, or long-term, linked to specific goals, strategies, and expectations.

## FACTORS AFFECTING INVESTMENT TIME HORIZONS

| RISK TOLERANCE | MARKET CONDITIONS |
|---|---|
| INVESTMENT GOALS | TYPES OF INVESTMENTS |
| AGE | INVESTOR'S KNOWLEDGE & EXPERIENCE |
| FINANCIAL STABILITY | |

# TIME PLAYS A CRUCIAL ROLE IN INVESTMENT

## TYPES OF INVESTMENT TIME HORIZONS

| DURATION | FOCUS | INVESTMENTS TYPE | PURPOSE |
|---|---|---|---|
| **SHORT-TERM** | | | |
| **Less than 3 Years** | Preserving Capital & Minimizing Risk | Cash, Money Market Funds, Short Term Bonds | Sinking Fund with a set financial goal |
| **MID-TERM** | | | |
| **3 TO 10 Years** | Slightly more Risk Taking | Mix of Bonds, Stocks and Diversified Assests | Education, Marriage etc. |
| **LONG-TERM** | | | |
| **More than 10 Years** | High Risk Tolerance | Stocks, Real Estate, Growth-Oriented Assets | Retirement, Buy Home (Asset) without Loan |

## OTHER IMPORTANT FACTORS

### COMPOUND INTEREST

Time is a key factor in the power of compound interest. The longer your money is invested, the more time it has to grow exponentially.

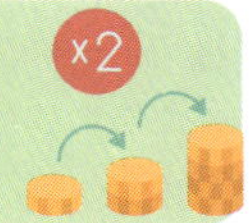


### VOLATILITY AND MARKET FLUCTUATIONS

Short-term fluctuations in the market are common, and they can be influenced by various factors. Over time, however, markets tend to move towards their long-term average trends. Longer the investment, more is the willingness to take the risk.

### DIVERSIFICATION

Diversifying your investments across different asset classes and sectors can help mitigate risks associated with specific market movements and improve the chances of overall portfolio growth over the long term.

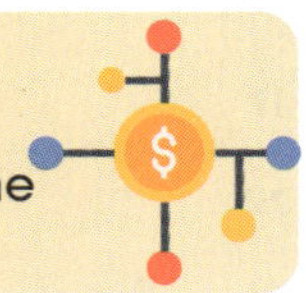

### INFLATION

Over time, inflation erodes the purchasing power of money. Investments that outpace inflation are crucial for preserving and growing wealth. Long-term investments in assets such as stocks and real estate have historically provided returns that outpace inflation.

In summary, time is a critical element in investment planning. It allows for the benefits of compounding, helps manage risk, and can enhance the effectiveness of various investment strategies. Investors should align their investment decisions with their financial goals and time horizons to optimize their chances of achieving long-term success.

# INVESTMENT ACCOUNT INFO

| No. | TYPE OF ACCOUNT | PLATFORM/ BANK | A/C HOLDER | A/C NUMBER |
|---|---|---|---|---|
| 1 | Fixed Deposit | | | |
| 2 | Shares / Demat | | | |
| 3 | Mutual Fund | | | |
| 4 | | | | |
| 5 | | | | |
| 6 | | | | |
| 7 | | | | |
| 8 | | | | |
| 9 | | | | |
| 10 | | | | |
| 11 | | | | |
| 12 | | | | |
| 13 | | | | |
| 14 | | | | |
| 15 | | | | |
| 16 | | | | |
| 17 | | | | |
| 18 | | | | |
| 19 | | | | |
| 20 | | | | |
| 21 | | | | |
| 22 | | | | |
| 23 | | | | |
| 24 | | | | |
| 25 | | | | |

*Notes*

"The stock market is designed to transfer money from the active to the patient." - Warren Buffett

| NO./ EMAIL ID | AMOUNT INVESTED | MATURITY | NOMINEE | ADDITIONAL INFO |
|---|---|---|---|---|
| | | | | |
| | | | | |
| | | | | |
| | | | | |
| | | | | |
| | | | | |
| | | | | |
| | | | | |
| | | | | |
| | | | | |
| | | | | |
| | | | | |
| | | | | |
| | | | | |
| | | | | |
| | | | | |
| | | | | |
| | | | | |
| | | | | |
| | | | | |
| | | | | |
| | | | | |
| | | | | |
| | | | | |
| | | | | |

*Notes*

"Making money is certainly the one addiction I cannot shake." - Felix Dennis

# INVESTMENT ACCOUNT INFO

| No. | TYPE OF ACCOUNT | PLATFORM/ BANK | A/C HOLDER | A/C NUMBER |
|---|---|---|---|---|
| 1 | Fixed Deposit | | | |
| 2 | Shares / Demat | | | |
| 3 | Mutual Fund | | | |
| 4 | | | | |
| 5 | | | | |
| 6 | | | | |
| 7 | | | | |
| 8 | | | | |
| 9 | | | | |
| 10 | | | | |
| 11 | | | | |
| 12 | | | | |
| 13 | | | | |
| 14 | | | | |
| 15 | | | | |
| 16 | | | | |
| 17 | | | | |
| 18 | | | | |
| 19 | | | | |
| 20 | | | | |
| 21 | | | | |
| 22 | | | | |
| 23 | | | | |
| 24 | | | | |
| 25 | | | | |

*Notes*

"Only buy something that you'd be perfectly happy to hold if the market shut down for 10 years." - Warren Buffett

| NO./ EMAIL ID | AMOUNT INVESTED | MATURITY | NOMINEE | ADDITIONAL INFO |
|---|---|---|---|---|
| | | | | |
| | | | | |
| | | | | |
| | | | | |
| | | | | |
| | | | | |
| | | | | |
| | | | | |
| | | | | |
| | | | | |
| | | | | |
| | | | | |
| | | | | |
| | | | | |
| | | | | |
| | | | | |
| | | | | |
| | | | | |
| | | | | |
| | | | | |
| | | | | |
| | | | | |
| | | | | |
| | | | | |
| | | | | |

*Notes*

"Diversification is protection against ignorance. It makes little sense if you know what you are doing." - Warren Buffett

# FIXED DEPOSIT LADDERING

FD laddering is a method in which you divide your entire investment amount among various FDs with varying maturities. Instead of putting all your money into one FD, you can build a ladder of FDs with varied maturity periods.

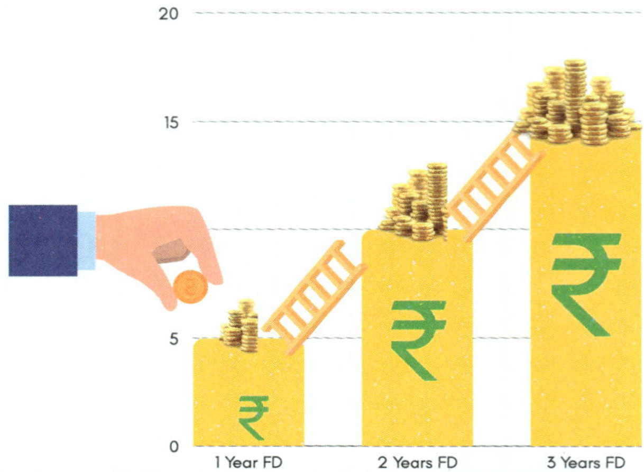


## CREATING AN FD LADDER INVOLVES THE FOLLOWING STEPS

1. **Determine your investment amount:** Decide how much money you want to invest in FDs.
2. **Select your FD tenures:** Choose the maturity dates for each FD.
3. **Invest in multiple FDs:** Split your investment into multiple FDs, each with a different maturity date. For example, if you have Rs 3 lakh, instead of investing it as a lump sum for 3 years, you could split it into 3 FDs of Rs 1 lakh each, the 1st for 1 year, the 2nd for 2 years, and the 3rd for 3 years.
4. **Reinvest matured FDs:** At the end of the first year, renew the matured FD for 3 years, creating the next rung. The following year, the FD with the 2-year tenure matures, and you reinvest it for 3 years, creating another rung.

This strategy creates a ladder of FDs, providing liquidity at the end of every year and potentially optimizing returns. Remember, it's always a good idea to consult with a financial advisor for personalized guidance based on your specific circumstances.

## BENEFITS OF FD LADDERING

- Optimized Returns
- Improved Liquidity
- Reduced Risk
- Opportunity for Better Rates
- Minimized Opportunity Loss

Disclaimer: This page designed by Muneem Khaata, is purely for educational purposes only. And not a financial advisory.

# GOLD INVESTMENT

## PHYSICAL/SOLID FORM OF GOLD

GOLD COINS OR BARS/BULLIONS

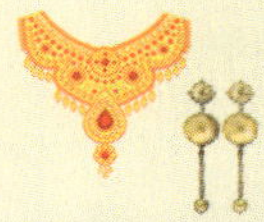

JEWELLERY

### BENEFITS

Tangible Asset

Long Term Investment

Tax saving

Gives a Sense of Security

Value Is Unaffected by Market

## E-FORM/ ONLINE GOLD

Below are some options which lets you invest in Gold without physical ownership.

### GOLD ETF

- **Directly linked:** Performance of the metal Gold.
- **Passively managed** investment instrument.
- Invests in gold of 99.5% purity.
- **1 unit gold ETF**= Ranging from 0.01 gm of physical gold to 1 gm
- **TAX**: As per Slab Rate
- **Avg. Returns:** 10% interest
- **Extra Cost:** Approx 0.5%to 1%

### SOVERIGN GOLD BOND

- Govt backed investment issued by RBI.
- **Where to Buy?**

Available at commercial banks, SHCIL, designated Post-Offices & Stock Exchanges like NSE & BSE (Groww, Upstox & Zerodha)

- **Duration:** 8 years Lockin
- **TAX:** No Tax on maturity
- **Avg. Returns:** 10%+2.5% Interest
- **Extra Cost:** 0

### GOLD FUNDS

- **Actively Managed** by fund managers & only invest in gold **via Gold ETFs**
- Each fund is managed on the basis of the **investment objective.**
- **TAX:**As per Slab Rate
- **Avg. Returns:** 10%
- **Extra Cost:** Approx. 0.5%to 1%

## IMPORTANCE OF DIVERSE GOLD INVESTMENT

- Gold ETFs and Gold Funds provide investors with an easy way of diversifying their portfolios beyond equity and debt. As has been observed in the recent past, the gold and equity markets are often found to follow a see-saw pattern, i.e. when one is low, the other is high, and vice versa. This provides a sufficient hedge to your portfolio.

- Keeping in mind the facts and need one can decide the type of investment to be made in gold.

# GOLD ASSET TRACKER

| No. | FORM OF GOLD | SOURCE | (GMS) | BUY DATE | RATE | REMARK |
|---|---|---|---|---|---|---|
| 1 | Jewellery | Jeweller name | | | | |
| 2 | Coins | | | | | |
| 3 | Gold ETF | | | | | |
| 4 | | | | | | |
| 5 | | | | | | |
| 6 | | | | | | |
| 7 | | | | | | |
| 8 | | | | | | |
| 9 | | | | | | |
| 10 | | | | | | |
| 11 | | | | | | |
| 12 | | | | | | |
| 13 | | | | | | |
| 14 | | | | | | |
| 15 | | | | | | |
| 16 | | | | | | |
| 17 | | | | | | |
| 18 | | | | | | |
| 19 | | | | | | |
| 20 | | | | | | |
| 21 | | | | | | |
| 22 | | | | | | |
| 23 | | | | | | |
| 24 | | | | | | |
| 25 | | | | | | |

*Notes*

"The key to making money is to stay invested." - Suze Orman

# GOLD ASSET TRACKER

| No. | FORM OF GOLD | SOURCE | (GMS) | BUY DATE | RATE | REMARK |
|---|---|---|---|---|---|---|
| 1 | Jewellery | Jeweller name | | | | |
| 2 | Coins | | | | | |
| 3 | Gold ETF | | | | | |
| 4 | | | | | | |
| 5 | | | | | | |
| 6 | | | | | | |
| 7 | | | | | | |
| 8 | | | | | | |
| 9 | | | | | | |
| 10 | | | | | | |
| 11 | | | | | | |
| 12 | | | | | | |
| 13 | | | | | | |
| 14 | | | | | | |
| 15 | | | | | | |
| 16 | | | | | | |
| 17 | | | | | | |
| 18 | | | | | | |
| 19 | | | | | | |
| 20 | | | | | | |
| 21 | | | | | | |
| 22 | | | | | | |
| 23 | | | | | | |
| 24 | | | | | | |
| 25 | | | | | | |

*Notes*

"We have gold because we cannot trust governments." - Herbert Hoover

# GOVT INVESTMENTS

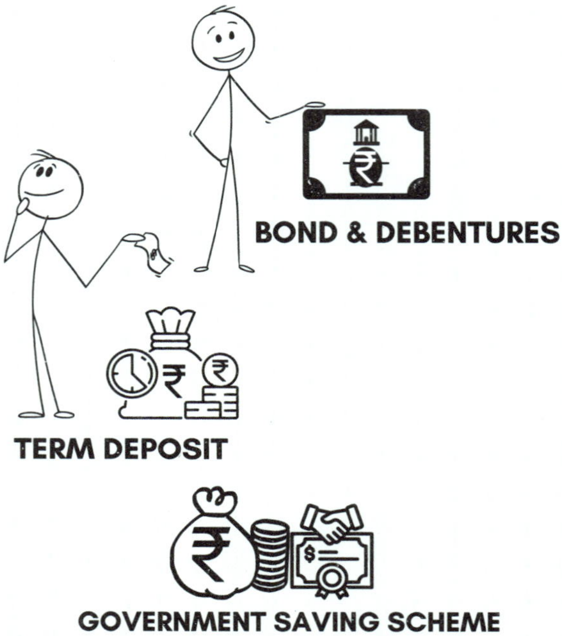

## SHORT-LIST OF GOVERNMENT INVESTMENT SCHEMES

- Public Provident Fund (PPF)
- National Savings Certificate (NSC)
- Sukanya Samriddhi Yojana (SSY)
- National Pension Scheme (NPS)
- Sovereign Gold Bonds (SGB)
- Atal Pension Yojana
- Pradhan Mantri Jan Dhan Yojana
- Kisan Vikas Patra (KVP)
- Post Office Time Deposit Account
- Post Office Monthly Income Scheme (POMIS)

Disclaimer: This page designed by Muneem Khaata, is purely for educational purposes only. And not a financial advisory.

# MEANINGS IN OF IMPORTANT INVESTMENT TERMS

## THEMATIC MUTUAL FUNDS

Thematic funds are equity funds that invest in companies focused on specific themes like manufacturing, innovation, and pharma to capitalize on growth opportunities in those sectors.

## COMMODITY

Commodity stocks involve companies extracting and processing natural resources for sale. There are two types of commodities: hard (gold, oil, copper, and natural gas) and soft.

## SEBI

The Securities and Exchange Board of India, commonly known as SEBI. It regulates commodities and securities markets in India similar to how RBI oversees banks.

## HEDGING

Hedging is a risk management strategy employed to offset losses in investments by taking an opposite position in a related asset. Hedging requires one to pay money for the protection it provides, known as the premium.
Hedging strategies typically involve derivatives, such as options and futures contracts.

## FUTURE & OPTIONS

A futures contract involves buying or selling an asset at a set price on a specific date. While an options contract grants the investor the right, but not the obligation, to buy or sell assets at a predetermined price by a specific expiry date.

## IPO

When a company opts to offer a portion of its ownership to the public for the first time, it launches an Initial Public Offering (IPO).

## MARKET CAPITALIZATION

Market capitalization, or market cap, represents the total value of a company's shares owned by shareholders. It is calculated by multiplying the number of outstanding shares by the current market price per share. **There are 3 types of Market Caps.**

### LARGE CAP COMPANIES:

- *Market capitalization* ***over Rs. 20,000 cr.***
- On the stock exchanges, these companies are ranked from 1 to 100.Well established with significant market share.
- Examples: HDFC Bank, TCS.

### MID CAP COMPANIES:

- *Market capitalization* ***between Rs. 5,000 cr. and Rs. 20,000 cr.***
- These companies have the potential to become a large cap in a few years and have enough finance to survive harsh economic conditions. Potential to become large cap.
- Example: Bajaj Finance.

### SMALL CAP COMPANIES:

- *Market capitalization* ***less than Rs. 2,000 cr.***
- Include start-ups and early-stage companies.
- Riskier with higher growth potential.
- Example: Suven Life Sciences.

# GOVT. SCHEMES AND

| No. | TYPE OF SCHEME | SOURCE | SCHEME NAME | CERTIFICATE/ ACCOUNT NO. |
|---|---|---|---|---|
| 1 | Bonds | | | |
| 2 | PPF | | | |
| 3 | | | | |
| 4 | | | | |
| 5 | | | | |
| 6 | | | | |
| 7 | | | | |
| 8 | | | | |
| 9 | | | | |
| 10 | | | | |
| 11 | | | | |
| 12 | | | | |
| 13 | | | | |
| 14 | | | | |
| 15 | | | | |
| 16 | | | | |
| 17 | | | | |
| 18 | | | | |
| 19 | | | | |
| 20 | | | | |
| 21 | | | | |
| 22 | | | | |
| 23 | | | | |
| 24 | | | | |
| 25 | | | | |

*Notes*

"When growth is slower-than-expected, stocks go down. When inflation is higher-than-expected, bonds go down. When inflation is lower-than-expected, bonds go up." - Ray Dalio

# BONDS INFORMATION

| AMOUNT | ISSUED DATE | MATURITY | NOMINEE | PURPOSE | REMARKS |
| --- | --- | --- | --- | --- | --- |
| | | | | Marriage | |
| | | | | Retirement | |
| | | | | | |
| | | | | | |
| | | | | | |
| | | | | | |
| | | | | | |
| | | | | | |
| | | | | | |
| | | | | | |
| | | | | | |
| | | | | | |
| | | | | | |
| | | | | | |
| | | | | | |
| | | | | | |
| | | | | | |
| | | | | | |
| | | | | | |
| | | | | | |
| | | | | | |
| | | | | | |
| | | | | | |
| | | | | | |
| | | | | | |

*Notes*

"Bonds as an asset class will always be needed, and not just by insurance companies and pension funds but by aging boomers." - Bill Gross

# GOVT. SCHEMES AND

| No. | TYPE OF SCHEME | SOURCE | SCHEME NAME | CERTIFICATE/ ACCOUNT NO. |
|---|---|---|---|---|
| 1 | Bonds | | | |
| 2 | PPF | | | |
| 3 | | | | |
| 4 | | | | |
| 5 | | | | |
| 6 | | | | |
| 7 | | | | |
| 8 | | | | |
| 9 | | | | |
| 10 | | | | |
| 11 | | | | |
| 12 | | | | |
| 13 | | | | |
| 14 | | | | |
| 15 | | | | |
| 16 | | | | |
| 17 | | | | |
| 18 | | | | |
| 19 | | | | |
| 20 | | | | |
| 21 | | | | |
| 22 | | | | |
| 23 | | | | |
| 24 | | | | |
| 25 | | | | |

*Notes*

"With a good perspective on history, we can have a better understanding of the past and present, and thus a clear vision of the future." - Carlos Slim Helu

# BONDS INFORMATION

| AMOUNT | ISSUED DATE | MATURITY | NOMINEE | PURPOSE | REMARKS |
|---|---|---|---|---|---|
| | | | | Marriage | |
| | | | | Retirement | |
| | | | | | |
| | | | | | |
| | | | | | |
| | | | | | |
| | | | | | |
| | | | | | |
| | | | | | |
| | | | | | |
| | | | | | |
| | | | | | |
| | | | | | |
| | | | | | |
| | | | | | |
| | | | | | |
| | | | | | |
| | | | | | |
| | | | | | |
| | | | | | |
| | | | | | |
| | | | | | |
| | | | | | |
| | | | | | |
| | | | | | |

*Notes*

"The stock market is filled with individuals who know the price of everything, but the value of nothing."
- Phillip Fisher

# FOREIGN PORTFOLIO
## Tracker

BROKER/PLATFORM

ACCOUNT INFO:

START DATE

START CAPITAL

Foreign investment is when a domestic investor decides to purchase ownership of an asset in a foreign country.

| No. | BUY DATE | COMPANY | INDEX | SYMBOL | SECTOR | BUY/SELL |
|---|---|---|---|---|---|---|
| 1 | | | | | | |
| 2 | | | | | | |
| 3 | | | | | | |
| 4 | | | | | | |
| 5 | | | | | | |
| 6 | | | | | | |
| 7 | | | | | | |
| 8 | | | | | | |
| 9 | | | | | | |
| 10 | | | | | | |
| 11 | | | | | | |
| 12 | | | | | | |
| 13 | | | | | | |
| 14 | | | | | | |
| 15 | | | | | | |
| 16 | | | | | | |
| 17 | | | | | | |
| 18 | | | | | | |
| 19 | | | | | | |
| 20 | | | | | | |

“There's never a perfect time to invest in stocks or the stock market, but there is a right time and a wrong time!” - James Pattersenn Jr,

YEAR/MONTH

USERNAME/ EMAIL:

TPIN/ CODE:

PASSWORD:

OTHER INFO:

| PRICE | NO. OF SHARES | FEES | SELL DATE | GAIN/LOSS |
|---|---|---|---|---|
| | | | | |
| | | | | |
| | | | | |
| | | | | |
| | | | | |
| | | | | |
| | | | | |
| | | | | |
| | | | | |
| | | | | |
| | | | | |
| | | | | |
| | | | | |
| | | | | |
| | | | | |
| | | | | |
| | | | | |
| | | | | |
| | | | | |
| | | | | |

"An investment in knowledge pays the best interest." - Benjamin Franklin

# FOREIGN PORTFOLIO
Tracker

BROKER/PLATFORM

ACCOUNT INFO:

START DATE

START CAPITAL

Foreign investment is when a domestic investor decides to purchase ownership of an asset in a foreign country.

| No. | BUY DATE | COMPANY | INDEX | SYMBOL | SECTOR | BUY/SELL |
|---|---|---|---|---|---|---|
| 1 | | | | | | |
| 2 | | | | | | |
| 3 | | | | | | |
| 4 | | | | | | |
| 5 | | | | | | |
| 6 | | | | | | |
| 7 | | | | | | |
| 8 | | | | | | |
| 9 | | | | | | |
| 10 | | | | | | |
| 11 | | | | | | |
| 12 | | | | | | |
| 13 | | | | | | |
| 14 | | | | | | |
| 15 | | | | | | |
| 16 | | | | | | |
| 17 | | | | | | |
| 18 | | | | | | |
| 19 | | | | | | |
| 20 | | | | | | |

"In investing, what is comfortable is rarely profitable." - Robert Arnott

YEAR/MONTH

USERNAME/ EMAIL:

TPIN/ CODE:

PASSWORD:

OTHER INFO:

| PRICE | NO. OF SHARES | FEES | SELL DATE | GAIN/LOSS |
|---|---|---|---|---|
| | | | | |
| | | | | |
| | | | | |
| | | | | |
| | | | | |
| | | | | |
| | | | | |
| | | | | |
| | | | | |
| | | | | |
| | | | | |
| | | | | |
| | | | | |
| | | | | |
| | | | | |
| | | | | |
| | | | | |
| | | | | |
| | | | | |
| | | | | |

"How many millionaires do you know who have become wealthy by investing in savings accounts? I rest my case." - Robert G. Allen

# DEFINATION OF STOCK MARKET TERMS

**STOCK**
A stock is a unit of ownership in a company. When you buy a stock, you become a partial owner of the company.

**SHARE**
A share is a unit of stock. For example, if a company has 100 shares, each share represents 1/100 ownership of the company.

**STOCK EXCHANGE**
A stock exchange is a market where stocks and other securities are traded. The Bombay Stock Exchange (BSE) and the National Stock Exchange of India (NSE) are the two stock exchanges currently operating in India.

**DEMAT ACCOUNT**
Demat account stores fi nancial assets, including shares, ETFs, sovereign gold bonds, mutual funds, bonds, ULIPs, etc. You can create a Demat account with a broker.

**NIFTY 50**
The Nifty 50 group is the 50 biggest and most active equities on the NSE. Investors might use it to determine the general market mood. National Stock Exchange and Fifty are combined to form the phrase "Nifty 50.".

**SENSEX 30 OR SENSEX**
Sensex is the BSE's flagship index. It consists of the 30 largest, most traded securities on the BSE. The sensitivity index is what is referred to as "Sensex" informally.

**BEAR MARKET**
A market where prices are falling. Bear Market denotes a falling trend in the total market values of the equities listed on the stock exchange. A certain stock is said to be "bearish" if its price rapidly declines.

**BULL MARKET**
A market where prices are rising. A bull market is the polar opposite of a bear market. It signifies that the market is rising. It indicates that the overall market values of the shares are increasing.

**PORTFOLIO**
Portfolio refers to an investor's assortment of holdings. One stock or several securities may be included in an investor's portfolio. It includes various financial securities, including stocks, bonds, futures, and options.

**INTRADAY TRADING & LONG-TERM TRADING**
Intraday trading, also called day trading, is the buying and selling of stocks and other financial instruments within the same day.
Long-term trading helps you save on taxes. Most short-term traders pay around 20%-30% tax on capital gains, while long-term capital gains are charged a tax of only 5%-15%.

SELL BUY

Disclaimer: This page designed by Muneem Khaata, is purely for educational purposes only. And not a financial advisory.

# MEANINGS IN SHORT FOR INVESTMENT TERMS

## NAV: Net Asset Value

The performance of a mutual fund is indicated by its NAV per unit, which changes daily based on the fund's total assets and liabilities.
The NAV calculation formula is:

**NAV = (Total Assets - Total Liabilities) / Total Number of Units.**

If you buy 100 units of a mutual fund at Rs 1000 with a Net Asset Value (NAV) of 10 rupees, your asset value will be Rs 1000. If the NAV increases to Rs 15, your asset value will rise to Rs 1500.

## P/E RATIO

Price to Earnings Ratio is the ratio of share price of a stock to its earnings per share (EPS). It provides indication whether a stock at its current market price is expensive or cheap.

$$\text{P/E RATIO} = \frac{\text{MARKET PRICE PER SHARE PRICE}}{\text{EARNINGS PER SHARE}}$$

## EBIDTA

EBITDA, or **Earnings Before Interest, Taxes, Depreciation, and Amortization**, is an alternate measure of profitability to net income. By including depreciation and amortization as well as taxes and debt payment costs, EBITDA attempts to represent the cash profit generated by the company's operations.

## LOCK-IN PERIOD

- Lock in period or lock up period refers to that period for which investments cannot be sold or redeemed.
- Lock in periods are commonly used for hedge funds, IPOs of private equity, start-ups and few mutual funds.
- On the expiry of the lock in period, one must not withdraw the funds immediately.

## BRICS CURRENCY

BRICS nations (Brazil, Russia, India, China, South Africa) aim to create a new reserve currency to challenge the dominance of the US dollar in the international financial system.
The potential currency is still under review and development.

## CRYPTOCURRENCY

A cryptocurrency is a form of virtual or digital asset distributed across a huge number of computers based on a network. It is typically a decentralized digital fund designed to be over the net. It is not governed or regulated by any central authority or government.

Disclaimer: This page designed by Muneem Khaata, is purely for educational purposes only. And not a financial advisory.

# STOCKS PORTFOLIO
## Tracker

| BROKER/PLATFORM | ACCOUNT INFO: |
|---|---|
| START DATE | START CAPITAL |

| No. | BUY DATE | COMPANY | INDEX | SYMBOL | SECTOR | BUY/SELL |
|---|---|---|---|---|---|---|
| 1 | | | | | | |
| 2 | | | | | | |
| 3 | | | | | | |
| 4 | | | | | | |
| 5 | | | | | | |
| 6 | | | | | | |
| 7 | | | | | | |
| 8 | | | | | | |
| 9 | | | | | | |
| 10 | | | | | | |
| 11 | | | | | | |
| 12 | | | | | | |
| 13 | | | | | | |
| 14 | | | | | | |
| 15 | | | | | | |
| 16 | | | | | | |
| 17 | | | | | | |
| 18 | | | | | | |
| 19 | | | | | | |
| 20 | | | | | | |

"I will tell you how to become rich. Close the doors. Be fearful when others are greedy. Be greedy when others are fearful." - Warren Buffett

**YEAR/MONTH**

**USERNAME/ EMAIL:**

**TPIN/ CODE:**

**PASSWORD:**

**OTHER INFO:**

| PRICE | NO. OF SHARES | FEES | SELL DATE | GAIN/LOSS |
|---|---|---|---|---|
| | | | | |
| | | | | |
| | | | | |
| | | | | |
| | | | | |
| | | | | |
| | | | | |
| | | | | |
| | | | | |
| | | | | |
| | | | | |
| | | | | |
| | | | | |
| | | | | |
| | | | | |
| | | | | |
| | | | | |
| | | | | |
| | | | | |
| | | | | |

"The stock market is filled with individuals who know the price of everything, but the value of nothing." - Phillip Fisher

# STOCKS PORTFOLIO Tracker

| BROKER/PLATFORM | ACCOUNT INFO: |
|---|---|
| START DATE | START CAPITAL |

| No. | BUY DATE | COMPANY | INDEX | SYMBOL | SECTOR | BUY/SELL |
|---|---|---|---|---|---|---|
| 1 | | | | | | |
| 2 | | | | | | |
| 3 | | | | | | |
| 4 | | | | | | |
| 5 | | | | | | |
| 6 | | | | | | |
| 7 | | | | | | |
| 8 | | | | | | |
| 9 | | | | | | |
| 10 | | | | | | |
| 11 | | | | | | |
| 12 | | | | | | |
| 13 | | | | | | |
| 14 | | | | | | |
| 15 | | | | | | |
| 16 | | | | | | |
| 17 | | | | | | |
| 18 | | | | | | |
| 19 | | | | | | |
| 20 | | | | | | |

"Investing should be more like watching paint dry or watching grass grow. If you want excitement, take $800 and go to Las Vegas." - Paul Samuelson

YEAR/MONTH

USERNAME/ EMAIL:

TPIN/ CODE:

PASSWORD:

OTHER INFO:

| PRICE | NO. OF SHARES | FEES | SELL DATE | GAIN/LOSS |
|---|---|---|---|---|
| | | | | |
| | | | | |
| | | | | |
| | | | | |
| | | | | |
| | | | | |
| | | | | |
| | | | | |
| | | | | |
| | | | | |
| | | | | |
| | | | | |
| | | | | |
| | | | | |
| | | | | |
| | | | | |
| | | | | |
| | | | | |
| | | | | |
| | | | | |

"The stock market is filled with individuals who know the price of everything, but the value of nothing." - Phillip Fisher

# STOCKS PORTFOLIO
## Tracker

BROKER/PLATFORM

ACCOUNT INFO:

START DATE

START CAPITAL

| No. | BUY DATE | COMPANY | INDEX | SYMBOL | SECTOR | BUY/SELL |
|---|---|---|---|---|---|---|
| 1 | | | | | | |
| 2 | | | | | | |
| 3 | | | | | | |
| 4 | | | | | | |
| 5 | | | | | | |
| 6 | | | | | | |
| 7 | | | | | | |
| 8 | | | | | | |
| 9 | | | | | | |
| 10 | | | | | | |
| 11 | | | | | | |
| 12 | | | | | | |
| 13 | | | | | | |
| 14 | | | | | | |
| 15 | | | | | | |
| 16 | | | | | | |
| 17 | | | | | | |
| 18 | | | | | | |
| 19 | | | | | | |
| 20 | | | | | | |

"I will tell you how to become rich. Close the doors. Be fearful when others are greedy. Be greedy when others are fearful." - Warren Buffett

YEAR/MONTH

USERNAME/ EMAIL:

TPIN/ CODE:

PASSWORD:

OTHER INFO:

| PRICE | NO. OF SHARES | FEES | SELL DATE | GAIN/LOSS |
|---|---|---|---|---|
| | | | | |
| | | | | |
| | | | | |
| | | | | |
| | | | | |
| | | | | |
| | | | | |
| | | | | |
| | | | | |
| | | | | |
| | | | | |
| | | | | |
| | | | | |
| | | | | |
| | | | | |
| | | | | |
| | | | | |
| | | | | |
| | | | | |
| | | | | |

"The stock market is filled with individuals who know the price of everything, but the value of nothing."
- Phillip Fisher

# POWER OF COMPOUNDING

Power of compounding refers to capability of an investment to generate earnings, not only on the principal amount, by also on the interest earned over time. There are a number of investment options where the power of compounding is used and the interest earned is added to your invested funds

## COMPOUNDING WORKS WONDERS WHEN YOU START EARLY

Began investing at age 25 with Rs. 6000 in the first year. **She increased her investment by 10% annually.**

Began investing at age 40 with Rs. 15000 in the first year. **She increased her investment by 15% annually.**

| | | Mrs. GUPTA | Mrs. SEN |
|---|---|---|---|
| START YEAR | | 1980 | 1995 |
| Period | | 35 Years | 20 Years |
| 1st Year Investment | | Rs. 6000 | Rs. 15,000 |
| Investment Increased Annually By | | 10% | 10% |
| TOTAL INVESTMENT | | Rs. 16.26 Lakhs | Rs. 15.37 Lakhs |
| ASSURED RETURN @ | 8% | Rs. 39.95 Lakhs | Rs. 25.08 Lakhs |
| | 11% | Rs. 62.83 Lakhs | Rs. 31.14 Lakhs |
| | 14% | Rs. 105.00 Lakhs | Rs. 39.34 Lakhs |

**NOTICE HOW**

@14% Growth rate, Mrs. Gupta's investment could fetch Rs. 105 Crores as against Mrs. Sens investment value of 39.94 Lakhs though there is not much difference in the total investment made by both.

**Designed by theindianplanner for educative purpose Only.**

$$A = P(1 + r/n)^{(nt)}$$

Where:
A = the future value of the investment, including interest
P = the principal amount (initial investment)
r = the annual interest rate
n = the number of times that interest is compounded per year
t = the number of years the money is invested

This formula takes into account both the initial principal amount and the accumulated interest over time, based on the compounding frequency.

Reference from www.etmoney.com/learn/personal-finance/what-is-power-of-compounding-meaning-benefit/

Disclaimer: This page designed by Muneem Khaata, is purely for educational purposes only. And not a financial advisory.

# MUTUAL FUNDS

A mutual fund is a pool of money managed by a professional Fund Manager. It is a trust that collects money from a number of investors who share a common investment objective and invests the same in equities, bonds, money market instruments and/or other securities

Mutual fund portfolios can be **actively managed or passively managed.**

- An **actively managed** fund means a fund manager has more involvement in the decision making, is more active in looking after which stocks and bonds go in and out of a mutual fund portfolio and when.
- In **passively managed** funds, the fund manager cannot decide the movement of the underlying assets. It is also known as **ETF**, short for exchange-traded fund. here the manager pools money from investors to further invest in securities, including stocks, bonds, commodities, etc.

## TYPES OF MUTUAL FUND

**BASED ON BELOW FACTORS**

**RISK**
- LOW RISK
- LOW TO MODERATE
- MODERATE
- MODERATELY HIGH
- HIGH
- VERY HIGH

**STRUCTURE**
- OPEN ENDED FUNDS
- CLOSE ENDED FUNDS

**ASSET CLASS**

**EQUITY FUNDS**
- Multi-Cap
- Large Cap
- Large & Mid Cap
- Mid Cap
- Small Cap
- Value Funds
- Contra Funds
- Sectoral / Theme
- ELSS Funds

**ETF'S / GOLD**
- Equity ETFs
- Debt ETFs
- Gold ETFs
- Gold MFs
- FOFs Domestic
- FOFs Overseas

**HYBRID FUNDS**
- Conservative Hybrid
- Balanced Hybrid
- Aggressive Hybrid
- Dynamic Asset Allocation
- Multi-Asset Allocation
- Arbitrage Fund
- Equity Saving Fund

**DEBT FUNDS**
- Overnight Funds
- Liquid Funds
- Ultra Short-Term Funds
- Money Market Funds
- Short Duration Funds
- Medium Duration
- Long Duration
- Dynamic Bond Funds
- Corporate Bond Funds
- Credit Risk Funds
- Banking & PSU Funds
- Target Maturity Funds

**OBJECTIVE**
- GROWTH
- TAX SAVING
- INCOME
- RETIREMENT
- LIQUID

**SPECIALITY**
- INDEX FUND
- FUNDS OF FUNDS
- COMMODITY
- ASSET ALLOCATION
- RETIREMENT
- CHILDREN

# MUTUAL FUND PORTFOLIO
Tracker

| BROKER/PLATFORM | ACCOUNT INFO: |
|---|---|
| START DATE | START CAPITAL |

| No. | START DATE | SCHEME NAME/TRANSACTION TYPE | FOLIO NUMBER | ORDER DATE |
|---|---|---|---|---|
| 1 | | | | |
| 2 | | | | |
| 3 | | | | |
| 4 | | | | |
| 5 | | | | |
| 6 | | | | |
| 7 | | | | |
| 8 | | | | |
| 9 | | | | |
| 10 | | | | |
| 11 | | | | |
| 12 | | | | |
| 13 | | | | |
| 14 | | | | |
| 15 | | | | |
| 16 | | | | |
| 17 | | | | |
| 18 | | | | |
| 19 | | | | |
| 20 | | | | |
| 21 | | | | |
| 22 | | | | |
| 23 | | | | |
| 24 | | | | |
| 25 | | | | |

"Waiting helps you as an investor and a lot of people just can't stand to wait. If you didn't get the deferred-gratification gene, you've got to work very hard to overcome that."- Charlie Munger

YEAR/MONTH

USERNAME/ EMAIL:

TPIN/ CODE:

PASSWORD:

OTHER INFO:

| AMOUNT/ SIP | TARGET % | END DATE | NOMINEE | AIM OF INVESTMENT | REMARK |
|---|---|---|---|---|---|
| | | | | | |
| | | | | | |
| | | | | | |
| | | | | | |
| | | | | | |
| | | | | | |
| | | | | | |
| | | | | | |
| | | | | | |
| | | | | | |
| | | | | | |
| | | | | | |
| | | | | | |
| | | | | | |
| | | | | | |
| | | | | | |
| | | | | | |
| | | | | | |
| | | | | | |
| | | | | | |
| | | | | | |
| | | | | | |
| | | | | | |
| | | | | | |
| | | | | | |

"To make the most of your money, I recommend sticking with mutual funds that don't charge a commission when you buy or sell."- Suze Orman

# MUTUAL FUND PORTFOLIO
Tracker

| BROKER/PLATFORM | ACCOUNT INFO: |
|---|---|
| START DATE | START CAPITAL |

| No. | START DATE | SCHEME NAME/TRANSACTION TYPE | FOLIO NUMBER | ORDER DATE |
|---|---|---|---|---|
| 1 | | | | |
| 2 | | | | |
| 3 | | | | |
| 4 | | | | |
| 5 | | | | |
| 6 | | | | |
| 7 | | | | |
| 8 | | | | |
| 9 | | | | |
| 10 | | | | |
| 11 | | | | |
| 12 | | | | |
| 13 | | | | |
| 14 | | | | |
| 15 | | | | |
| 16 | | | | |
| 17 | | | | |
| 18 | | | | |
| 19 | | | | |
| 20 | | | | |
| 21 | | | | |
| 22 | | | | |
| 23 | | | | |
| 24 | | | | |
| 25 | | | | |

"How many millionaires do you know who have become wealthy by investing in savings accounts? I rest my case." - Robert G. Allen

YEAR/MONTH

USERNAME/ EMAIL:

TPIN/ CODE:

PASSWORD:

OTHER INFO:

| AMOUNT/ SIP | TARGET % | END DATE | NOMINEE | AIM OF INVESTMENT | REMARK |
|---|---|---|---|---|---|
| | | | | | |
| | | | | | |
| | | | | | |
| | | | | | |
| | | | | | |
| | | | | | |
| | | | | | |
| | | | | | |
| | | | | | |
| | | | | | |
| | | | | | |
| | | | | | |
| | | | | | |
| | | | | | |
| | | | | | |
| | | | | | |
| | | | | | |
| | | | | | |
| | | | | | |
| | | | | | |
| | | | | | |
| | | | | | |
| | | | | | |
| | | | | | |
| | | | | | |

"The individual investor should act consistently as an investor and not as a speculator." - Ben Graham

# MUTUAL FUND PORTFOLIO
Tracker

BROKER/PLATFORM

ACCOUNT INFO:

START DATE

START CAPITAL

| No. | START DATE | SCHEME NAME/TRANSACTION TYPE | FOLIO NUMBER | ORDER DATE |
|---|---|---|---|---|
| 1 | | | | |
| 2 | | | | |
| 3 | | | | |
| 4 | | | | |
| 5 | | | | |
| 6 | | | | |
| 7 | | | | |
| 8 | | | | |
| 9 | | | | |
| 10 | | | | |
| 11 | | | | |
| 12 | | | | |
| 13 | | | | |
| 14 | | | | |
| 15 | | | | |
| 16 | | | | |
| 17 | | | | |
| 18 | | | | |
| 19 | | | | |
| 20 | | | | |
| 21 | | | | |
| 22 | | | | |
| 23 | | | | |
| 24 | | | | |
| 25 | | | | |

"Mutual funds have historically offered safety and diversification. And they spare you the responsibility of picking individual stocks."- Ron Chernow

YEAR/MONTH

USERNAME/ EMAIL:

TPIN/ CODE:

PASSWORD:

OTHER INFO:

| AMOUNT/ SIP | TARGET % | END DATE | NOMINEE | AIM OF INVESTMENT | REMARK |
|---|---|---|---|---|---|
| | | | | | |
| | | | | | |
| | | | | | |
| | | | | | |
| | | | | | |
| | | | | | |
| | | | | | |
| | | | | | |
| | | | | | |
| | | | | | |
| | | | | | |
| | | | | | |
| | | | | | |
| | | | | | |
| | | | | | |
| | | | | | |
| | | | | | |
| | | | | | |
| | | | | | |
| | | | | | |
| | | | | | |
| | | | | | |
| | | | | | |
| | | | | | |
| | | | | | |

"Mutual funds were created to make investing easy, so consumers wouldn't have to be burdened with picking individual stocks."- Scott Cook

# CRYPTOCURRENCY
## Tracker

| BROKER/PLATFORM | ACCOUNT INFO: |
|---|---|
| **START DATE** | **START CAPITAL** |

| DATE | DESCRIPTION | PURCHASE AMOUNT (-) |
|---|---|---|
| | | |
| | | |
| | | |
| | | |
| | | |
| | | |
| | | |
| | | |
| | | |
| | | |
| | | |
| | | |
| | | |
| | | |
| | | |
| | | |
| | | |
| | | |
| | | |
| | | |
| | | |

If you don't believe it or don't get it, I don't have the time to try to convince you, sorry. - Satoshi Nakamoto

**YEAR/MONTH**

**USERNAME/ EMAIL:**

**TPIN/ CODE:**

**PASSWORD:**

**OTHER INFO:**

| FEES (-) | SELL AMOUNT (+) | TOTAL | REMARKS |
|---|---|---|---|
| | | | |
| | | | |
| | | | |
| | | | |
| | | | |
| | | | |
| | | | |
| | | | |
| | | | |
| | | | |
| | | | |
| | | | |
| | | | |
| | | | |
| | | | |
| | | | |
| | | | |
| | | | |
| | | | |
| | | | |
| | | | |

We don't prognosticate macroeconomic factors, we're looking at our companies from a bottom-up perspective on their long-run prospects of returning." - Mellody Hobson

# INVESTING IN REAL ESTATE

Investing in real estate is viewed as a lucrative opportunity in India, propelled by the country's continuous growth. However there are more than one ways to invest in real estate.

## HOW

- PROPERTIES
- REITS
- MUTUAL FUNDS & ETFs
- PRIVATE FUNDS

## BENEFITS

## TYPES

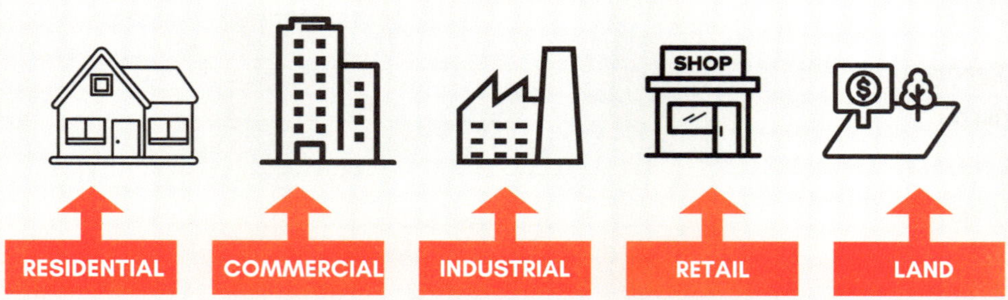


"Real estate cannot be lost or stolen, nor can it be carried away. Purchased with common sense, paid for in full, and managed with reasonable care, it is about the safest investment in the world."
Franklin D. Roosevelt

# PROPERTY INFORMATION

**OWNER NAME:**

REGISTERING AUTHORITY: ____________________

TYPE OF PROPERTY: ____________________

RERA NO: ____________________

REGISTRATION NO: ____________ REG DATE: ____________

CO-OWNER NAME.: ____________ CONTACT ____________

PURPOSE OF PROPERTY: ________ SOURCE OF INVESTMENT: SELF ______ OR GIFT ______

AREA RATE/SQ FT: ________ RERA CARPET AREA: ________ TOTAL AREA: ________

DATE OF PURCHASE: ____________ PROPERTY COST: ____________

PURCHASE DETAILS: FULL DOWNPAYMENT/ LOAN / EMI: ____________

____________________

PROPERTY POSSESION DATE: ____________ PROPERTY STATUS: RENTAL/STAY ____________

FIRST OWNER: ____________ NOMINEE: ____________

AGENT/ BROKER: ____________ CONTACT: ____________

TAX DETAILS: ____________________

PROPERTY ADDRESS: ____________________

____________________

____________________

REGN ADDRESS: ____________________

NOTES/ EXTRA INFO: ____________________

____________________

____________________

MONTHLY MAINTENANCE: ____________________

RENTAL YIELD: ____________________

RENOVATION/REPAIRS EXPENSES: ____________________

INTEREST PAID ON LOAN: ____________________

*Notes* ....................

....................

"Owning a home is a keystone of wealth... both financial affluence and emotional security."

– Suze Orman, financial advisor

# PROPERTY INFORMATION

**OWNER NAME:**

REGISTERING AUTHORITY: ____________________

TYPE OF PROPERTY: ____________________

RERA NO: ____________________

REGISTRATION NO: ____________ REG DATE: ____________

CO-OWNER NAME.: ____________ CONTACT ____________

PURPOSE OF PROPERTY: ________ SOURCE OF INVESTMENT: SELF ______ OR GIFT ______

AREA RATE/SQ FT: ________ RERA CARPET AREA: ________ TOTAL AREA: ________

DATE OF PURCHASE: ____________ PROPERTY COST: ____________

PURCHASE DETAILS: FULL DOWNPAYMENT/ LOAN / EMI: ____________________

____________________

PROPERTY POSSESION DATE: ____________ PROPERTY STATUS: RENTAL/STAY ____________

FIRST OWNER: ____________ NOMINEE: ____________

AGENT/ BROKER: ____________ CONTACT: ____________

TAX DETAILS: ____________________

PROPERTY ADDRESS: ____________________

____________________

____________________

REGN ADDRESS: ____________________

NOTES/ EXTRA INFO: ____________________

____________________

____________________

MONTHLY MAINTENANCE: ____________________

RENTAL YIELD: ____________________

RENOVATION/REPAIRS EXPENSES: ____________________

INTEREST PAID ON LOAN: ____________________

*Notes* ....................

"Now, one thing I tell everyone is learn about real estate. Repeat after me: real estate provides the highest returns, the greatest values and the least risk". - Armstrong Williams

# PROPERTY INFORMATION

**OWNER NAME:**

REGISTERING AUTHORITY: ____________________

TYPE OF PROPERTY: ____________________

RERA NO: ____________________

REGISTRATION NO: ______________ REG DATE: ______________

CO-OWNER NAME.: ______________ CONTACT ______________

PURPOSE OF PROPERTY: __________ SOURCE OF INVESTMENT: SELF ______ OR GIFT ______

AREA RATE/SQ FT: ________ RERA CARPET AREA: ________ TOTAL AREA: ________

DATE OF PURCHASE: ______________ PROPERTY COST: ______________

PURCHASE DETAILS: FULL DOWNPAYMENT/ LOAN / EMI: ____________________

____________________

PROPERTY POSSESION DATE: ______________ PROPERTY STATUS: RENTAL/STAY ______________

FIRST OWNER: ______________ NOMINEE: ______________

AGENT/ BROKER: ______________ CONTACT: ______________

TAX DETAILS: ____________________

PROPERTY ADDRESS: ____________________

____________________

____________________

REGN ADDRESS: ____________________

NOTES/ EXTRA INFO: ____________________

____________________

____________________

MONTHLY MAINTENANCE: ____________________

RENTAL YIELD: ____________________

RENOVATION/REPAIRS EXPENSES: ____________________

INTEREST PAID ON LOAN: ____________________

*Notes* ....................

....................

"Landlords grow rich in their sleep." – John Stuart Mill

# PROPERTY INFORMATION

**OWNER NAME:**

REGISTERING AUTHORITY: ____________________

TYPE OF PROPERTY: ____________________

RERA NO: ____________________

REGISTRATION NO: ____________________ REG DATE: ____________________

CO-OWNER NAME.: ____________________ CONTACT ____________________

PURPOSE OF PROPERTY: ____________ SOURCE OF INVESTMENT: SELF ________ OR GIFT ________

AREA RATE/SQ FT: __________ RERA CARPET AREA: __________ TOTAL AREA: __________

DATE OF PURCHASE: ____________________ PROPERTY COST: ____________________

PURCHASE DETAILS: FULL DOWNPAYMENT/ LOAN / EMI: ____________________

____________________

PROPERTY POSSESION DATE: ____________ PROPERTY STATUS: RENTAL/STAY ____________

FIRST OWNER: ____________________ NOMINEE: ____________________

AGENT/ BROKER: ____________________ CONTACT: ____________________

TAX DETAILS: ____________________

PROPERTY ADDRESS: ____________________

____________________

____________________

REGN ADDRESS: ____________________

NOTES/ EXTRA INFO: ____________________

____________________

____________________

MONTHLY MAINTENANCE: ____________________

RENTAL YIELD: ____________________

RENOVATION/REPAIRS EXPENSES: ____________________

INTEREST PAID ON LOAN: ____________________

*Notes* ....................

....................

"Buying real estate is not only the best way, the quickest way, the safest way, but the only way to become wealthy." - Marshall Field, entrepreneur.

# PROPERTY INFORMATION

**OWNER NAME:**

**REGISTERING AUTHORITY:** ____________________

**TYPE OF PROPERTY:** ____________________

**RERA NO:** ____________________

**REGISTRATION NO:** ____________ **REG DATE:** ____________

**CO-OWNER NAME.:** ____________ **CONTACT** ____________

**PURPOSE OF PROPERTY:** ________ **SOURCE OF INVESTMENT: SELF** ______ **OR GIFT** ______

**AREA RATE/SQ FT:** ______ **RERA CARPET AREA:** ______ **TOTAL AREA:** ______

**DATE OF PURCHASE:** ____________ **PROPERTY COST:** ____________

**PURCHASE DETAILS: FULL DOWNPAYMENT/ LOAN / EMI:** ____________

____________________

**PROPERTY POSSESION DATE:** ____________ **PROPERTY STATUS: RENTAL/STAY** ____________

**FIRST OWNER:** ____________ **NOMINEE:** ____________

**AGENT/ BROKER:** ____________ **CONTACT:** ____________

**TAX DETAILS:** ____________________

**PROPERTY ADDRESS:** ____________________

____________________

____________________

**REGN ADDRESS:** ____________________

**NOTES/ EXTRA INFO:** ____________________

____________________

____________________

**MONTHLY MAINTENANCE:** ____________________

**RENTAL YIELD:** ____________________

**RENOVATION/REPAIRS EXPENSES:** ____________________

**INTEREST PAID ON LOAN:** ____________________

*Notes* ....................

....................

"Owning a home is a keystone of wealth... both financial affluence and emotional security."
- Suze Orman, financial advisor

# PROPERTIES OVERVIEW

| No. | PROPERTY NAME | PROPERTY AREA/LOCATION | NAME OF OWNERS |
|---|---|---|---|
| 1 | | | |
| 2 | | | |
| 3 | | | |
| 4 | | | |
| 5 | | | |
| 6 | | | |
| 7 | | | |
| 8 | | | |
| 9 | | | |
| 10 | | | |
| 11 | | | |
| 12 | | | |
| 13 | | | |
| 14 | | | |
| 15 | | | |
| 16 | | | |
| 17 | | | |
| 18 | | | |
| 19 | | | |
| 20 | | | |

*Notes*

"There is a gigantic difference between earning a great deal of money and being rich." - Marlene Dietrich

# PROPERTIES OVERVIEW

| SOURCE | PURPOSE | NOMINEE/S OR HEIR |
|---|---|---|
| Gift | Live | |
| Inherited | Rent | |
| Self | | |
| | | |
| | | |
| | | |
| | | |
| | | |
| | | |
| | | |
| | | |
| | | |
| | | |
| | | |
| | | |
| | | |
| | | |
| | | |
| | | |
| | | |

*Notes*

"Buy land, they're not making it anymore." – Mark Twain

# PROPERTY RETURN

| No. | PROPERTY NAME | TYPE | START DATE | END DATE | TENTANT NAME | TENANT/ CONTACT |
|---|---|---|---|---|---|---|
| 1 | | | | | | |
| 2 | | | | | | |
| 3 | | | | | | |
| 4 | | | | | | |
| 5 | | | | | | |
| 6 | | | | | | |
| 7 | | | | | | |
| 8 | | | | | | |
| 9 | | | | | | |
| 10 | | | | | | |
| 11 | | | | | | |
| 12 | | | | | | |
| 13 | | | | | | |
| 14 | | | | | | |
| 15 | | | | | | |
| 16 | | | | | | |
| 17 | | | | | | |
| 18 | | | | | | |
| 19 | | | | | | |
| 20 | | | | | | |

*Notes*

"If we command our wealth, we shall be rich and free. If our wealth commands us, we are poor indeed." - Edmund Burke

# ON INVESTMENT

| RENTAL AMOUNT | MAINTENANCE | PROFIT/ YIELD | REMARKS |
|---|---|---|---|
| | | | |
| | | | |
| | | | |
| | | | |
| | | | |
| | | | |
| | | | |
| | | | |
| | | | |
| | | | |
| | | | |
| | | | |
| | | | |
| | | | |
| | | | |
| | | | |
| | | | |
| | | | |
| | | | |
| | | | |

*Notes*

"If you don't own a home, buy one. If you own a home, buy another one. If you own two homes, buy a third." - John Paulson

# START-UPS OR ENTERPRENEURSHIP

Entrepreneurship is the ability and readiness to develop, organize and run a business enterprise, along with any of its uncertainties in order to make a profit

## WHAT?

## WHY?

MAKE MONEY!

IMPORTANT

SOLVE PROBLEM FOR COMMUNITY!

FIND

## IDEAS

JOURNAL

What I need that I cannot find?

NEEDS

Of people around you

BRAINSTORM

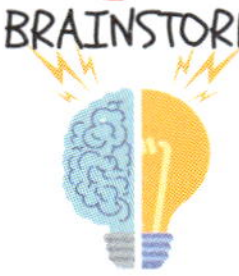

Create NEW Product

**FAMOUS INDIAN START-UPS**

- Pharma Easy
- Meesho
- Practo
- Digit
- Nykaa
- Zomato

# SIDE HUSTLE

A piece of work or a job that you get paid for doing in addition to doing your main job

- WORK FROM HOME: DIGITAL MARKETING
- WRITE A BOOK
- AFFLIATE MARKETING
- START A BLOG
- TUTOR ONLINE
- INFLUENCE MARKETING
- CLOUD KITCHEN
- PAID CONSULTATION
- DESIGNING

**BENEFITS**

- Earn more money
- Diversify Income
- Pursue Passion
- Can become Full time
- Help Other People
- Transition to another field
- Increase skill set
- Gives you inner peace

# FUNDING SOURCES & GOVT. INITIATIVE

## SOURCES OF START-UP FUNDING

SELF FUNDING

FAMILY & FRIENDS

VENTURE CAPITAL/ FAMILY OFFICES/PVT EQUITY

ANGEL INVESTOR

CROWD FUNDING

INCUBATORS & ACCELERATORS

GOVT. SCHEMES

DEBT LOAN

## GOVERNMENT SCHEMES

### GOVT. OF INDIA INITIATIVES

- STARTUP INDIA INITIATIVE
- MAHILA COIR YOJANA
- UDYAM SHAKTI PORTAL
- ASPIRE
- CREDIT GUARANTEE TRUST FUND
- SINGLE POINT REGISTRATION SCHEME
- PRADHAN MANTRI MUDHRA YOJNA
- VENTURE CAPITAL ASSISTANCE SCHEME
- ATAL INNOVATION MISSION
- THE STANDUP INDIA SCHEME
- RAW MATERIAL ASSISTANCE SCHEME
- DESIGN CLINIC SCHEME

**BENEFITS**

Financial assistance

Tax benefits

Encourages Women Entrepreneurs

Networking Opportunities

Easy Access to Vital Resources

Collateral Free Loan

**The final stage of a private corporation transitioning to a publicly traded company is the IPO stage.**

# BUSINESS INFORMATION

Name of the Business: ____________________

Owners Name: ____________________

Status/Designation: ____________________

Application No: ____________________

Registration Ceft/ Intimation Receipt No: ____________________

Nature of Business: ____________________

Establishment: Public or Pvt: ____________________

Category of Establishment: ____________________

Establishment Type: ____________________

Type of Organization: ____________________

Address: ____________________

____________________

No of Employees: ____________________

Aadhaar No: ____________________

PAN Card: ____________________

Business Insurance: ____________________

Description: ____________________

____________________

____________________

____________________

____________________

*Notes*

.......................................................................

.......................................................................

.......................................................................

.......................................................................

'Ideas are commodity. The execution of them is not.' – Michael Dell, CEO of Dell

# TRADEMARK / LOGO REGISTRATION

**Nature Of Application:** ______________________

**Application Filed as:** ______________________

**Fees:** ______________________

**Applicant: No.:** ______________________

**Name:** ______________________

**Address of Applicant:** ______________________

______________________

______________________

**Jurisdiction:** ______________________

**Address of Service:** ______________________

______________________

______________________

**Mobile No:** ______________ **Email Address:** ______________

**Nature of Applicant:** ______________________

**Legal Status:** ______________________

**Applicant's Agent (If Any):** ______________________

______________________

**Nature of Agent:** ______________________

**Registration No:** ______________________

**Mark Details:** ______________________

**Category of Marked Details:** ______________________

______________________

*Notes*

................................................

................................................

................................................

................................................

'There's nothing wrong with staying small. You can do big things with a small team.'

– Jason Fried, founder of Basecamp

# FUNDING SOURCES & DIFFERENT LEVELS OF INVESTORS

## HOW TO CHOOSE THE RIGHT TYPE OF FUNDING FOR YOUR STARTUP?

## TYPES OF FUNDING FOR YOUR STARTUP

| PRE-SEED | SEED STAGE | EARLY STAGE |
|---|---|---|
| • Laying foundation<br>• Ideation<br>• Testing & analysis | • Confirm product demand.<br>• Validate your Business Model<br>• Find right market solutions<br>• Make the right contacts.<br>• Rely on mulitple financial sources. | • Reaching the 1st round of venture capital funding<br>• Crafting Minimum viable product (MVP)<br>• Establish sizeable customer base.<br>• Steady stream of monthly revenue. |
| **FUNDING:**<br>• Start-up Owners<br>• Friends & Family | **FUNDING:**<br>• Personal Savings<br>• Credit Cards<br>• Angel Investors<br>• Venture Capital<br>• Crowdfunding | **FUNDING:**<br>• Angel Capital<br>• Venture Capital<br>• Accelerators<br><br>**LOANS**<br>• Bank Loans<br>• Grants<br>• Crowd Funding |

# FUNDING SOURCES & DIFFERENT LEVELS OF INVESTORS

## TYPES OF FUNDING FOR YOUR STARTUP

| GROWTH STAGE | EXPANSION STAGE | EXIT |
|---|---|---|
| • Scale to bigger market<br>• Maintain long term profitability.<br>• Raising fund<br>• Expand team.<br>• Aim for healthy growth.<br>• Counting on the right people. | • Profitable & self-sufficient<br>• Aim to expand.<br>• Venture into the global market.<br>• Expand to other market segments.<br>• Rely on help, guidance, strategic partnerships.<br>• Consider acquisitions to accelerate expansions | • Expand by acquring more companies<br>• The possibility of selling<br>• Decide how to proceed<br>• The exit depends on your goals<br>• Plan an Exit Strategy |
| **FUNDING:**<br>• Venture Capital (Late Stage VC)<br>• Corporate Venture Loans<br>• Bank Loans<br>• Govt Loans | **FUNDING:**<br>• Mezzanine Financing Phase<br>• hedge fund groups,<br>• investment banks,<br>• private equity firms<br>• Late-stage venture capital companies | **FUNDING:**<br>• Late-Stage VCs<br>• Private Equity Firms<br>• Hedge Funds<br>• Banks<br>• Cash Out Strategy<br>• ESOP<br>• IPO |

# INTELLECTUAL PROPERTY

Intellectual property (IP) is a category of property that includes intangible creations of the human intellect.

**TYPES OF INTELLECTUAL PROPERTY RIGHTS**
In India, there are 7 types of intellectual property rights, namely - copyright, trademarks, patents, geographical indications, plant varieties, industrial designs and semiconductor integrated circuit layout designs.

## INTELLECTUAL PROPERTY RIGHT

**Name of the Owner:** ____________________

**Type Of Property:** ____________________

**Registration Date:** ____________________

**Details:** ____________________

*Notes*

"Intellectual property is the currency of the 21st century." - Mark Getty

# DIGITAL ASSETS

A digital asset is usually an item created and stored digitally, identifiable, discoverable, and valuable. As technology advances further into our personal and professional lives, the importance and popularity of digital assets have increased. Data, images, videos, written content, and other types have long been acknowledged as digital assets with ownership rights.

## DIGITAL ASSETS

**SOCIAL MEDIA**

**PERSONAL DATA**

**ONLINE TRADING**

**CRYPTOCURRENCY**

**MONETIZED ACCOUNTS**

**DATA BACKUP**

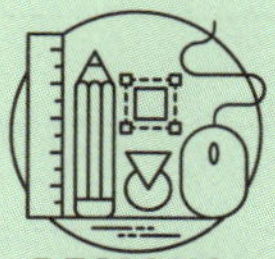

**DESIGNS**

**NFT**

## IMPORTANCE

### SENTIMENTAL VALUES

- Pictures & Video.
- Life Archived in the form of stories creates long last memories.
- A bridge to long distance relationship.
- Staying connected with old friends

### MONETIZED CONTENT

- YouTube for Videos
- Facebook & Instagram for Photos, Videos, content, business etc.
- Podcasting Audio content
- Linkedin professional growth
- Accounts with over 1 million followers earn from collaborations.
- They also create their brand image.

### PERSONAL & FINANCIAL DATA

- Online Banking, UPI, Trading is all digital nowadays.
- Digital Data is utmost important and can be considered as an asset.
- NFT & Cryptocurrency are a new era of digital currencies.
- Keeping a track of finances also involves documents in form of excel sheets & docs.

"Don't use social media to impress people; use it to impact people."- Dave Willis

# SOCIAL MEDIA ACCOUNT TRACKER

| No. | PLATFORM | ACCOUNT HANDLE | USERNAME | PASSWORD |
|---|---|---|---|---|
| 1. | YouTube Channel | | | |
| 2. | Intsagram | | | |
| 3. | Facebook | | | |
| 4. | | | | |
| 5. | | | | |
| 6. | | | | |
| 7. | | | | |
| 8. | | | | |
| 9. | | | | |
| 10. | | | | |
| 11. | | | | |
| 12. | | | | |
| 13. | | | | |
| 14. | | | | |
| 15. | | | | |
| 16. | | | | |
| 17. | | | | |
| 18. | | | | |
| 19. | | | | |
| 20. | | | | |

*Notes*

"Social Media is about the people! Not about your business. Provide for the people and the people will provide for you." - Matt Goulart.

# GIFTS TRACKER

| No. | OCCASSION | GIFT GIVER | RECEIVER | GIFT ITEM | REMARKS |
|---|---|---|---|---|---|
| 1 | | | | | |
| 2 | | | | | |
| 3 | | | | | |
| 4 | | | | | |
| 5 | | | | | |
| 6 | | | | | |
| 7 | | | | | |
| 8 | | | | | |
| 9 | | | | | |
| 10 | | | | | |
| 11 | | | | | |
| 12 | | | | | |
| 13 | | | | | |
| 14 | | | | | |
| 15 | | | | | |
| 16 | | | | | |
| 17 | | | | | |
| 18 | | | | | |
| 19 | | | | | |
| 20 | | | | | |
| 21 | | | | | |
| 22 | | | | | |
| 23 | | | | | |
| 24 | | | | | |
| 25 | | | | | |

"Financial peace isn't the acquisition of stuff. It's learning to live on less than you make, so you can give money back and have money to invest. You can't win until you do this." - Dave Ramsey

# GIFTS TRACKER

| No. | OCCASSION | GIFT GIVER | RECEIVER | GIFT ITEM | REMARKS |
|---|---|---|---|---|---|
| 1 | | | | | |
| 2 | | | | | |
| 3 | | | | | |
| 4 | | | | | |
| 5 | | | | | |
| 6 | | | | | |
| 7 | | | | | |
| 8 | | | | | |
| 9 | | | | | |
| 10 | | | | | |
| 11 | | | | | |
| 12 | | | | | |
| 13 | | | | | |
| 14 | | | | | |
| 15 | | | | | |
| 16 | | | | | |
| 17 | | | | | |
| 18 | | | | | |
| 19 | | | | | |
| 20 | | | | | |
| 21 | | | | | |
| 22 | | | | | |
| 23 | | | | | |
| 24 | | | | | |
| 25 | | | | | |

"Know what you own, and know why you own it." - Peter Lynch

# GIFTS TRACKER

| No. | OCCASSION | GIFT GIVER | RECEIVER | GIFT ITEM | REMARKS |
|---|---|---|---|---|---|
| 1 | | | | | |
| 2 | | | | | |
| 3 | | | | | |
| 4 | | | | | |
| 5 | | | | | |
| 6 | | | | | |
| 7 | | | | | |
| 8 | | | | | |
| 9 | | | | | |
| 10 | | | | | |
| 11 | | | | | |
| 12 | | | | | |
| 13 | | | | | |
| 14 | | | | | |
| 15 | | | | | |
| 16 | | | | | |
| 17 | | | | | |
| 18 | | | | | |
| 19 | | | | | |
| 20 | | | | | |
| 21 | | | | | |
| 22 | | | | | |
| 23 | | | | | |
| 24 | | | | | |
| 25 | | | | | |

"No one has ever become poor by giving." - Anne Frank

# ZAKAAT CALCULATIONS

| ZAKAAT PAYABLE ASSETS | |
|---|---|
| **ASSET** | **AMOUNT** |
| Gold (In any form) | |
| Silver (In any form) | |
| Cash in Hand or Bank | |
| Loans which are receivable | |
| Foreign Currency (@Indian Rate) | |
| Bonds | |
| Shares (@ actual rate) | |
| Fixed Deposits | |
| Amount deposited for future (Eg. Marriage , Haj, Education) | |
| Amount put with any other person as amaanaath | |
| Installments paid for BC (Chitthi) If the amount has not been received) | |
| Any kind of insurance amount paid (If its period is not ended) | |
| Amount invested in Finance | |
| Employees GPF, PPF, EPF (when received) | |
| Extra GPF by his own will | |
| Land or Flat etc. purchased for the purpose of business ( Real Estate) | |
| Amount paid as advance (for any purpose) | |
| Value of good held for sale (at selling price) | |
| Value of Goods given on credit | |
| Investment as a partnership in any business | |
| Value of raw material in factory or shop ( e.g. paper for xerox, in xerox shop etc.) | |
| **TOTAL** | |

**Attested By: Moulana Syed Ehsanuddin Sahab**
Compiled By: Md. Yasir Hussain Rasheedi Qasmi

| LIABILITIES | |
|---|---|
| **DEDUCTIBLES** | **AMOUNT** |
| Loans which are payable | |
| Maher of wife (if not paid) | |
| Balance Installments of BC (If the amount has been received) | |
| Salaries of employees & utility bills for the month | |
| Last year's Zakaath (If not paid) | |
| | |
| **TOTAL** | |

| ZAKAAT CALCULATION | |
|---|---|
| Total Value of Assets | |
| Total Deductions | |
| Zakaath Payable Amount | |
| Zakaath Payable = (Zakaath Payable amount *2.5%) | |
| **TOTAL** | |

**IMPORTANT RULES (MASA'EL)**

- Zakaath is obligatory on every Muslim (men or women) who possess 612 gm of silver or equivalent of cash or any other assests mentioned above, on the completion of one year.
- 2.5% of the total amount should be paid as Zakaath.
- Zakaath can be paid only to those Muslims who do not have 612gms of silver or any other equivalent amount of cash or assets mentioned above.
- It is mentioned in Quraan which are as follows: Faqeer (who does not have food even for a single time), Miskeen (Who has food which is enough only for one time), Muslim Prisoner, Indebted, In the way of Allah like Islamic Madarsa students etc., wayfarer (traveller) if in need.
- If anyone paid the zakaath to the person who possesses 612gms of silver or equivalent cash or any other assests more than daily needs, his zakaath is not valid. So, zakaath should be paid after deep verification of needy.
- Zakaath can't be paid to Sayyeds, Parents, grandparents, children, grandchildren etc. as well as husband can't pay zakaath to his wife and wife to her husband.
- Zakaath can be given to all relatives other than these.

**Important: Previous years zakaath which has not been paid till now must be paid immediately.**

"Zakat is a right that the poor have upon the rich" - Sahih Bukhari

# ZAKAT TRACKER

| No. | YEAR | EXPECTED ZAKAT (RS.) | ZAKAT GIVEN (RS.) | TO |
|---|---|---|---|---|
| 1 | | | | |
| 2 | | | | |
| 3 | | | | |
| 4 | | | | |
| 5 | | | | |
| 6 | | | | |
| 7 | | | | |
| 8 | | | | |
| 9 | | | | |
| 10 | | | | |
| 11 | | | | |
| 12 | | | | |
| 13 | | | | |
| 14 | | | | |
| 15 | | | | |
| 16 | | | | |
| 17 | | | | |
| 18 | | | | |
| 19 | | | | |
| 20 | | | | |
| 21 | | | | |
| 22 | | | | |
| 23 | | | | |
| 24 | | | | |
| 25 | | | | |

"The best charity is to pay Zakat on one's wealth" - Sahih Muslim

# CHARITY TRACKER

| No. | DATE | RECEIVER | AMOUNT | REMARKS/ OCCASSION |
|---|---|---|---|---|
| 1 | | | | |
| 2 | | | | |
| 3 | | | | |
| 4 | | | | |
| 5 | | | | |
| 6 | | | | |
| 7 | | | | |
| 8 | | | | |
| 9 | | | | |
| 10 | | | | |
| 11 | | | | |
| 12 | | | | |
| 13 | | | | |
| 14 | | | | |
| 15 | | | | |
| 16 | | | | |
| 17 | | | | |
| 18 | | | | |
| 19 | | | | |
| 20 | | | | |
| 21 | | | | |
| 22 | | | | |
| 23 | | | | |
| 24 | | | | |
| 25 | | | | |
| 26 | | | | |
| 27 | | | | |
| 28 | | | | |
| 29 | | | | |
| 30 | | | | |

It's not how much we give but how much love we put into giving. - Mother Teresa

# CHARITY TRACKER

| No. | DATE | RECEIVER | AMOUNT | REMARKS/ OCCASSION |
|---|---|---|---|---|
| 1 | | | | |
| 2 | | | | |
| 3 | | | | |
| 4 | | | | |
| 5 | | | | |
| 6 | | | | |
| 7 | | | | |
| 8 | | | | |
| 9 | | | | |
| 10 | | | | |
| 11 | | | | |
| 12 | | | | |
| 13 | | | | |
| 14 | | | | |
| 15 | | | | |
| 16 | | | | |
| 17 | | | | |
| 18 | | | | |
| 19 | | | | |
| 20 | | | | |
| 21 | | | | |
| 22 | | | | |
| 23 | | | | |
| 24 | | | | |
| 25 | | | | |
| 26 | | | | |
| 27 | | | | |
| 28 | | | | |
| 29 | | | | |
| 30 | | | | |

It's not how much we give but how much love we put into giving. - Mother Teresa

# EMERGENCY FUND VS SINKING FUND

**P.S. You need both!!!**

## EMERGENCY FUND

This is to prepare for an **unexpected** cost

**FOR EXAMPLE:**

- Job Loss
- Car Breakdown
- Furlough/Layoff
- Medical

**USE ONLY FOR EMERGENCIES**

**KEEP BOTH IN AN EASYACCESS SAVING ACCOUNT**

## SINKING FUND

This is to prepare for an **expected** cost

**FOR EXAMPLE:**

- Diwali/Christmas
- Birthdays/ Gifts
- Annual Car Cost
- Holidays

**USE FOR PLANNED PURCHASES**

@theindianplanner

# EMERGENCY FUND

## WHAT?

STASH OF JUST INCASE MONEY

## WHY?

UNXPECTED COST

LOOSE YOUR JOB

END UP IN ER

NEED EMERGENCY REPAIRS

**THUMB RULE**

SAVE 3 TO 6 MONTHS LIVING EXPENSES

## TIPS

SET UP AUTOSAVE

KEEP IN A SEPERATE SAVING A/C

DISNEYLAND HOLIDAY IS NOT AN EMERGENCY

1. Calculate your Emergency Savings Amount
2. Set an Emergency Fund Target
3. Start saving on monthly basis or as and when possible
4. And keep a track of your progress by marking on the thermometer here

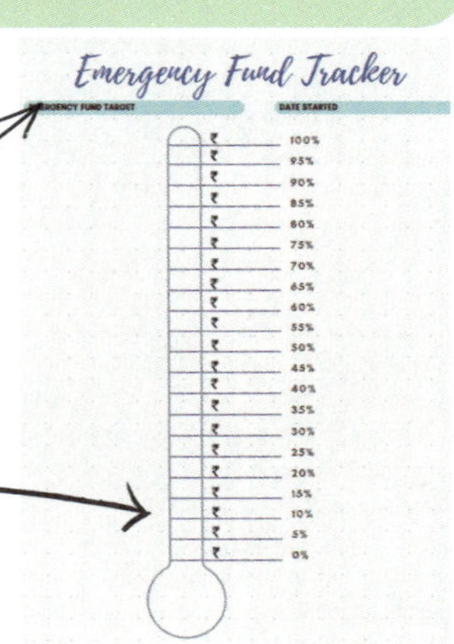


EMERGENCY SAVING TRACKER

# EMERGENCY FUND TRACKER

**FUND TARGET**

**DATE STARTED**

**ACCOUNT DETAILS**

| % | ₹ |
|---|---|
| 100% | ₹ |
| 95% | ₹ |
| 90% | ₹ |
| 85% | ₹ |
| 80% | ₹ |
| 75% | ₹ |
| 70% | ₹ |
| 65% | ₹ |
| 60% | ₹ |
| 55% | ₹ |
| 50% | ₹ |
| 45% | ₹ |
| 40% | ₹ |
| 35% | ₹ |
| 30% | ₹ |
| 25% | ₹ |
| 20% | ₹ |
| 15% | ₹ |
| 10% | ₹ |
| 5% | ₹ |
| 0% | ₹ |

Emergency fund is enough money to cover at least 6 to 12 months' worth of living expenses

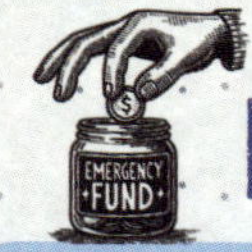


# EMERGENCY FUND TRACKER

**FUND TARGET**

**DATE STARTED**

**ACCOUNT DETAILS**

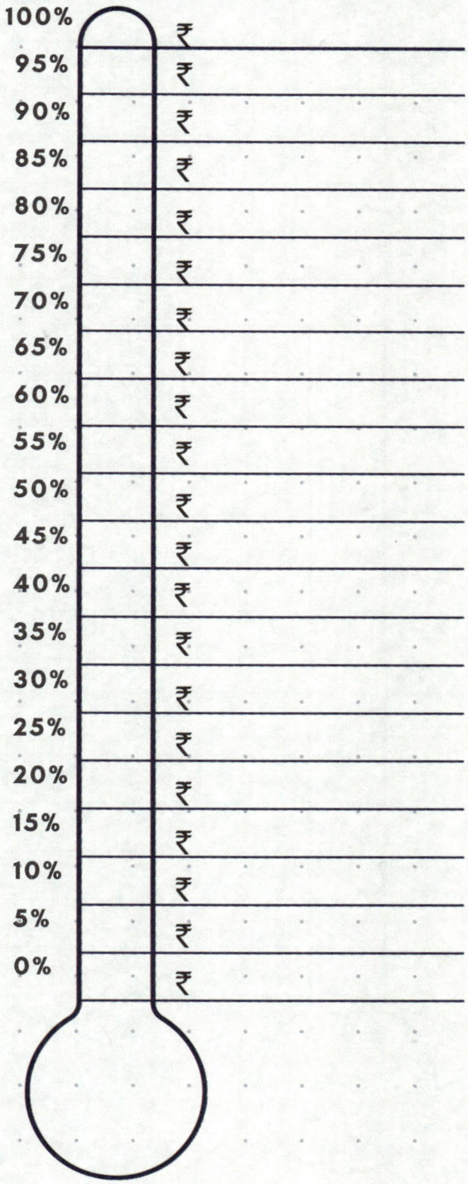


Emergency fund is enough money to cover at least 6 to 12 months' worth of living expenses

# EMERGENCY FUND TRACKER

**FUND TARGET**

**DATE STARTED**

**ACCOUNT DETAILS**

| | |
|---|---|
| 100% | ₹ |
| 95% | ₹ |
| 90% | ₹ |
| 85% | ₹ |
| 80% | ₹ |
| 75% | ₹ |
| 70% | ₹ |
| 65% | ₹ |
| 60% | ₹ |
| 55% | ₹ |
| 50% | ₹ |
| 45% | ₹ |
| 40% | ₹ |
| 35% | ₹ |
| 30% | ₹ |
| 25% | ₹ |
| 20% | ₹ |
| 15% | ₹ |
| 10% | ₹ |
| 5% | ₹ |
| 0% | ₹ |

Emergency fund is enough money to cover at least 6 to 12 months' worth of living expenses

# EMERGENCY FUND TRACKER

**FUND TARGET**

**DATE STARTED**

**ACCOUNT DETAILS**

| | |
|---|---|
| 100% | ₹ |
| 95% | ₹ |
| 90% | ₹ |
| 85% | ₹ |
| 80% | ₹ |
| 75% | ₹ |
| 70% | ₹ |
| 65% | ₹ |
| 60% | ₹ |
| 55% | ₹ |
| 50% | ₹ |
| 45% | ₹ |
| 40% | ₹ |
| 35% | ₹ |
| 30% | ₹ |
| 25% | ₹ |
| 20% | ₹ |
| 15% | ₹ |
| 10% | ₹ |
| 5% | ₹ |
| 0% | ₹ |

Emergency fund is enough money to cover at least 6 to 12 months' worth of living expenses

# SINKING FUNDS

## WHAT?

**SAVING SMALL AMOUNT FOR SHORT TERM GOALS**

## WHY?

**EXPECTED COSTS**

**PREPARE BUDGET LIKE A PRO**

**REDUCES STRESS ON POCKET**

**HELPS YOU STAY AWAY FROM DEBT**

**ACHIEVE BIG GOALS WITH EASE LIKE HOLIDAY**

- Sinking funds are money you set aside each month for specific savings goals. They allow you to save for infrequent expenses and plan for large expenses over time.

- Having sinking funds can help prevent you from withdrawing money from your emergency fund or going into debt to pay for things.

## 15 SINKING FUND IDEAS

### MAINTENANCE

- Buying New Car
- Home Renovations
- Gardening
- Replacing Old Appliances

### PERSONAL

- Hobbies
- Date Nights
- Pets
- Memberships
- Donations

### THE FUN STUFF

- Diwali/ Festival Gifts
- Wedding
- Vacation
- Clothing

### HEALTH

- Cosmetic Treatment
- Wellness
- Gym Membership

# SINKING FUND TRACKER

**GOAL:**

**AMOUNT:**

**GOAL DATE**

| DATE | AMOUNT | BALANCE |
|---|---|---|
| | | |
| | | |
| | | |
| | | |
| | | |
| | | |
| | | |
| | | |
| | | |
| | | |
| | | |
| | | |

**GOAL:**

**AMOUNT:**

**GOAL DATE:**

| DATE | AMOUNT | BALANCE |
|---|---|---|
| | | |
| | | |
| | | |
| | | |
| | | |
| | | |
| | | |
| | | |
| | | |
| | | |
| | | |
| | | |

**GOAL:**

**AMOUNT:**

**GOAL DATE**

| DATE | AMOUNT | BALANCE |
|---|---|---|
| | | |
| | | |
| | | |
| | | |
| | | |
| | | |
| | | |
| | | |
| | | |
| | | |
| | | |
| | | |

**GOAL:**

**AMOUNT:**

**GOAL DATE:**

| DATE | AMOUNT | BALANCE |
|---|---|---|
| | | |
| | | |
| | | |
| | | |
| | | |
| | | |
| | | |
| | | |
| | | |
| | | |
| | | |
| | | |

"A liability is anything that causes you to spend money and results in net value decreases." - Hendrith Smith

# SINKING FUNDS TRACKER

| DUE DATE/MONTH | GOAL AMOUNT | PUPORSE |
|---|---|---|
| | | |
| **DATE** | **AMOUNT** | **BALANCE** |
| | | |
| | | |
| | | |
| | | |
| | | |
| | | |
| | | |
| | | |
| | | |

| DUE DATE/MONTH | GOAL AMOUNT | PUPORSE |
|---|---|---|
| | | |
| **DATE** | **AMOUNT** | **BALANCE** |
| | | |
| | | |
| | | |
| | | |
| | | |
| | | |
| | | |
| | | |
| | | |

| DUE DATE/MONTH | GOAL AMOUNT | PUPORSE |
|---|---|---|
| | | |
| **DATE** | **AMOUNT** | **BALANCE** |
| | | |
| | | |
| | | |
| | | |
| | | |
| | | |
| | | |
| | | |
| | | |

| DUE DATE/MONTH | GOAL AMOUNT | PUPORSE |
|---|---|---|
| | | |
| **DATE** | **AMOUNT** | **BALANCE** |
| | | |
| | | |
| | | |
| | | |
| | | |
| | | |
| | | |
| | | |
| | | |

The most significant benefit of sinking funds is that they allow you to plan for expenses you know will pop up

# SINKING FUNDS TRACKER

| DUE DATE/MONTH | GOAL AMOUNT | PUPORSE |
|---|---|---|
| | | |
| **DATE** | **AMOUNT** | **BALANCE** |
| | | |
| | | |
| | | |
| | | |
| | | |
| | | |
| | | |
| | | |
| | | |

| DUE DATE/MONTH | GOAL AMOUNT | PUPORSE |
|---|---|---|
| | | |
| **DATE** | **AMOUNT** | **BALANCE** |
| | | |
| | | |
| | | |
| | | |
| | | |
| | | |
| | | |
| | | |
| | | |

| DUE DATE/MONTH | GOAL AMOUNT | PUPORSE |
|---|---|---|
| | | |
| **DATE** | **AMOUNT** | **BALANCE** |
| | | |
| | | |
| | | |
| | | |
| | | |
| | | |
| | | |
| | | |
| | | |

| DUE DATE/MONTH | GOAL AMOUNT | PUPORSE |
|---|---|---|
| | | |
| **DATE** | **AMOUNT** | **BALANCE** |
| | | |
| | | |
| | | |
| | | |
| | | |
| | | |
| | | |
| | | |
| | | |

he most significant benefit of sinking funds is that they allow you to plan for expenses you know will pop up

# SINKING FUNDS TRACKER

| FUND FOR | GOAL AMOUNT | DUE DATE |
|---|---|---|
| | | |

| DATE | AMOUNT | BALANCE |
|---|---|---|
| | | |
| | | |
| | | |
| | | |
| | | |
| | | |
| | | |
| | | |

VISUAL PROGRESS

| FUND FOR | GOAL AMOUNT | DUE DATE |
|---|---|---|
| | | |

| DATE | AMOUNT | BALANCE |
|---|---|---|
| | | |
| | | |
| | | |
| | | |
| | | |
| | | |
| | | |
| | | |

VISUAL PROGRESS

*Notes*

Every month, you'll save a certain amount of money for a specific purpose to use at a later date.

# SINKING FUNDS TRACKER

| FUND FOR | GOAL AMOUNT | DUE DATE |
| --- | --- | --- |
| | | |

| DATE | AMOUNT | BALANCE |
| --- | --- | --- |
| | | |
| | | |
| | | |
| | | |
| | | |
| | | |
| | | |
| | | |

VISUAL PROGRESS

| FUND FOR | GOAL AMOUNT | DUE DATE |
| --- | --- | --- |
| | | |

| DATE | AMOUNT | BALANCE |
| --- | --- | --- |
| | | |
| | | |
| | | |
| | | |
| | | |
| | | |
| | | |
| | | |

VISUAL PROGRESS

*Notes*

**Sinking Fund** is a fancy economic term for saving

# SINKING FUNDS TRACKER

| FUND FOR | GOAL AMOUNT | DUE DATE |
| --- | --- | --- |
| | | |

| DATE | AMOUNT | BALANCE |
| --- | --- | --- |
| | | |
| | | |
| | | |
| | | |
| | | |
| | | |
| | | |
| | | |

VISUAL PROGRESS

| FUND FOR | GOAL AMOUNT | DUE DATE |
| --- | --- | --- |
| | | |

| DATE | AMOUNT | BALANCE |
| --- | --- | --- |
| | | |
| | | |
| | | |
| | | |
| | | |
| | | |
| | | |
| | | |

VISUAL PROGRESS

*Notes*

"Money like emotions is something that you must control to keep your life on track." - Anonymous

# SINKING FUNDS TRACKER

| FUND FOR | GOAL AMOUNT | DUE DATE |
|---|---|---|
| | | |

| DATE | AMOUNT | BALANCE | VISUAL PROGRESS |
|---|---|---|---|
| | | | |
| | | | |
| | | | |
| | | | |
| | | | |
| | | | |
| | | | |
| | | | |

| FUND FOR | GOAL AMOUNT | DUE DATE |
|---|---|---|
| | | |

| DATE | AMOUNT | BALANCE | VISUAL PROGRESS |
|---|---|---|---|
| | | | |
| | | | |
| | | | |
| | | | |
| | | | |
| | | | |
| | | | |
| | | | |

*Notes*

A sinking fund is a pot of money created by setting aside money regularly to pay for planned yearly expenses.

# SINKING FUNDS TRACKER

| SAVINGS FOR: | SAVINGS FOR: |
|---|---|
| TARGET AMOUNT: | TARGET AMOUNT: |
| GOAL DATE: | GOAL DATE: |

| NO | DATE | AMOUNT | BALANCE |
|---|---|---|---|
| 1 | | | |
| 2 | | | |
| 3 | | | |
| 4 | | | |
| 5 | | | |
| 6 | | | |
| 7 | | | |
| 8 | | | |
| 9 | | | |
| 10 | | | |
| 11 | | | |
| 12 | | | |
| 13 | | | |
| 14 | | | |
| 15 | | | |
| 16 | | | |
| 17 | | | |
| 18 | | | |
| 19 | | | |
| 20 | | | |
| 21 | | | |
| 22 | | | |
| 23 | | | |
| 24 | | | |
| 25 | | | |

| NO | DATE | AMOUNT | BALANCE |
|---|---|---|---|
| 1 | | | |
| 2 | | | |
| 3 | | | |
| 4 | | | |
| 5 | | | |
| 6 | | | |
| 7 | | | |
| 8 | | | |
| 9 | | | |
| 10 | | | |
| 11 | | | |
| 12 | | | |
| 13 | | | |
| 14 | | | |
| 15 | | | |
| 16 | | | |
| 17 | | | |
| 18 | | | |
| 19 | | | |
| 20 | | | |
| 21 | | | |
| 22 | | | |
| 23 | | | |
| 24 | | | |
| 25 | | | |

*Notes*

A sinking fund is an account containing money set aside to pay off a debt or bond.

# SINKING FUNDS TRACKER

SAVINGS FOR:

TARGET AMOUNT:

GOAL DATE:

| NO | DATE | AMOUNT | BALANCE |
|---|---|---|---|
| 1 | | | |
| 2 | | | |
| 3 | | | |
| 4 | | | |
| 5 | | | |
| 6 | | | |
| 7 | | | |
| 8 | | | |
| 9 | | | |
| 10 | | | |
| 11 | | | |
| 12 | | | |
| 13 | | | |
| 14 | | | |
| 15 | | | |
| 16 | | | |
| 17 | | | |
| 18 | | | |
| 19 | | | |
| 20 | | | |
| 21 | | | |
| 22 | | | |
| 23 | | | |
| 24 | | | |
| 25 | | | |

SAVINGS FOR:

TARGET AMOUNT:

GOAL DATE:

| NO | DATE | AMOUNT | BALANCE |
|---|---|---|---|
| 1 | | | |
| 2 | | | |
| 3 | | | |
| 4 | | | |
| 5 | | | |
| 6 | | | |
| 7 | | | |
| 8 | | | |
| 9 | | | |
| 10 | | | |
| 11 | | | |
| 12 | | | |
| 13 | | | |
| 14 | | | |
| 15 | | | |
| 16 | | | |
| 17 | | | |
| 18 | | | |
| 19 | | | |
| 20 | | | |
| 21 | | | |
| 22 | | | |
| 23 | | | |
| 24 | | | |
| 25 | | | |

*Notes*

Having sinking funds can help prevent you from withdrawing money from your emergency fund or going into debt to pay for things.

# SINKING FUNDS TRACKER

**SAVINGS FOR:**

**TARGET AMOUNT:**

**GOAL DATE:**

| NO | DATE | AMOUNT | BALANCE |
|---|---|---|---|
| 1 | | | |
| 2 | | | |
| 3 | | | |
| 4 | | | |
| 5 | | | |
| 6 | | | |
| 7 | | | |
| 8 | | | |
| 9 | | | |
| 10 | | | |
| 11 | | | |
| 12 | | | |
| 13 | | | |
| 14 | | | |
| 15 | | | |
| 16 | | | |
| 17 | | | |
| 18 | | | |
| 19 | | | |
| 20 | | | |
| 21 | | | |
| 22 | | | |
| 23 | | | |
| 24 | | | |
| 25 | | | |

**SAVINGS FOR:**

**TARGET AMOUNT:**

**GOAL DATE:**

| NO | DATE | AMOUNT | BALANCE |
|---|---|---|---|
| 1 | | | |
| 2 | | | |
| 3 | | | |
| 4 | | | |
| 5 | | | |
| 6 | | | |
| 7 | | | |
| 8 | | | |
| 9 | | | |
| 10 | | | |
| 11 | | | |
| 12 | | | |
| 13 | | | |
| 14 | | | |
| 15 | | | |
| 16 | | | |
| 17 | | | |
| 18 | | | |
| 19 | | | |
| 20 | | | |
| 21 | | | |
| 22 | | | |
| 23 | | | |
| 24 | | | |
| 25 | | | |

*Notes*

A healthy sinking fund eliminates the need for bodies corporate and owner's corporations to borrow funds.

LIABILITIES
TAX
LOAN
CREDIT CARD
BILL
DEBT
850

DEBT

# WHY NOTING DOWN LIABILITY IS IMPORTANT?

Tracking personal debts or personal liability is crucial for several reasons, as it fosters healthy financial relationships and ensures financial transparency. Here are some key reasons for maintaining a record of your personal debts.

### FINANCIAL PLANNING

It helps with financial planning by setting aside funds for repayment, avoiding financial stress or unexpected budget issues.

### CLARITY AND ACCOUNTABILITY

Keeping records of personal debts helps avoid misunderstandings between borrowers and lenders by documenting the amount owed, repayment terms, and related conditions.

### LEGAL COMPLIANCE

Personal debts might be governed by legal regulations in certain situations. Maintaining a record helps ensure that both parties comply with legal obligations, safeguarding the rights and interests of all individuals concerned.

### MAINTAINING RELATIONSHIPS

Tracking personal debts promotes trust, transparency, and reduces conflicts by clarifying borrowed or lent money with friends, family, or acquaintances.

### AVOIDANCE OF INTEREST AND PENALTIES

Tracking debts prevents late payments, avoiding interest charges. Timely repayment maintains a good credit score.

### DOCUMENTATION FOR TAX PURPOSES

In specific cases, personal loans might have tax consequences. Keeping accurate records of loans can act as proof for tax purposes, like claiming interest deductions.

### FINANCIAL AWARENESS

Monitoring personal debts boosts financial awareness, allowing individuals to evaluate the overall debt & make informed decisions about borrowing or lending money.

### SETTING PRIORITIES

Understanding outstanding debts helps prioritize repayments based on factors like interest rates & urgency to address important financial obligations first.

### BUILDING GOOD FINANCIAL HABITS

Tracking personal debts regularly promotes responsible financial habits by encouraging critical thinking about financial decisions and timely repayment.

### PREVENTING OVERBORROWING

Maintaining a clear record of debts helps individuals evaluate borrowing capacity, avoiding excessive debt accumulation and financial instability.

In conclusion, monitoring personal debts fosters financial responsibility, transparency and positive relationships. It lays the groundwork for successful financial management and empowers individuals to make well-informed choices regarding their financial health.

# IT INFORMATION

ACCOUNT HOLDER:

PAN CARD:

AADHAAR CARD:

| No. | YEAR | DATE | TAXABLE INCOME | TAX PAID | TAX RETURN | ACKNOWLEDGEMENT NO. |
|---|---|---|---|---|---|---|
| 1 | | | | | | |
| 2 | | | | | | |
| 3 | | | | | | |
| 4 | | | | | | |
| 5 | | | | | | |
| 6 | | | | | | |
| 7 | | | | | | |
| 8 | | | | | | |
| 9 | | | | | | |
| 10 | | | | | | |
| 11 | | | | | | |
| 12 | | | | | | |
| 13 | | | | | | |
| 14 | | | | | | |
| 15 | | | | | | |
| 16 | | | | | | |
| 17 | | | | | | |
| 18 | | | | | | |
| 19 | | | | | | |
| 20 | | | | | | |
| 21 | | | | | | |
| 22 | | | | | | |
| 23 | | | | | | |
| 24 | | | | | | |
| 25 | | | | | | |

*Notes*

"There is a gigantic difference between earning a great deal of money and being rich." - Marlene Dietrich

# IT INFORMATION

ACCOUNT HOLDER:

PAN CARD:

AADHAAR CARD:

| No. | YEAR | DATE | TAXABLE INCOME | TAX PAID | TAX RETURN | ACKNOWLEDGEMENT NO. |
|---|---|---|---|---|---|---|
| 1 | | | | | | |
| 2 | | | | | | |
| 3 | | | | | | |
| 4 | | | | | | |
| 5 | | | | | | |
| 6 | | | | | | |
| 7 | | | | | | |
| 8 | | | | | | |
| 9 | | | | | | |
| 10 | | | | | | |
| 11 | | | | | | |
| 12 | | | | | | |
| 13 | | | | | | |
| 14 | | | | | | |
| 15 | | | | | | |
| 16 | | | | | | |
| 17 | | | | | | |
| 18 | | | | | | |
| 19 | | | | | | |
| 20 | | | | | | |
| 21 | | | | | | |
| 22 | | | | | | |
| 23 | | | | | | |
| 24 | | | | | | |
| 25 | | | | | | |

*Notes*

"When there is an income tax, the just man will pay more and the unjust less on the same amount of income." - Plato

# IT INFORMATION

ACCOUNT HOLDER:

PAN CARD:

AADHAAR CARD:

| No. | YEAR | DATE | TAXABLE INCOME | TAX PAID | TAX RETURN | ACKNOWLEDGEMENT NO. |
|---|---|---|---|---|---|---|
| 1 | | | | | | |
| 2 | | | | | | |
| 3 | | | | | | |
| 4 | | | | | | |
| 5 | | | | | | |
| 6 | | | | | | |
| 7 | | | | | | |
| 8 | | | | | | |
| 9 | | | | | | |
| 10 | | | | | | |
| 11 | | | | | | |
| 12 | | | | | | |
| 13 | | | | | | |
| 14 | | | | | | |
| 15 | | | | | | |
| 16 | | | | | | |
| 17 | | | | | | |
| 18 | | | | | | |
| 19 | | | | | | |
| 20 | | | | | | |
| 21 | | | | | | |
| 22 | | | | | | |
| 23 | | | | | | |
| 24 | | | | | | |
| 25 | | | | | | |

*Notes*

"I would like to electrocute everyone who uses the word 'fair' in connection with income tax policies." - William F. Buckley, Jr.

# IT INFORMATION

ACCOUNT HOLDER:

PAN CARD:

AADHAAR CARD:

| No. | YEAR | DATE | TAXABLE INCOME | TAX PAID | TAX RETURN | ACKNOWLEDGEMENT NO. |
|---|---|---|---|---|---|---|
| 1 | | | | | | |
| 2 | | | | | | |
| 3 | | | | | | |
| 4 | | | | | | |
| 5 | | | | | | |
| 6 | | | | | | |
| 7 | | | | | | |
| 8 | | | | | | |
| 9 | | | | | | |
| 10 | | | | | | |
| 11 | | | | | | |
| 12 | | | | | | |
| 13 | | | | | | |
| 14 | | | | | | |
| 15 | | | | | | |
| 16 | | | | | | |
| 17 | | | | | | |
| 18 | | | | | | |
| 19 | | | | | | |
| 20 | | | | | | |
| 21 | | | | | | |
| 22 | | | | | | |
| 23 | | | | | | |
| 24 | | | | | | |
| 25 | | | | | | |

*Notes*

"There's just one thing I can't figure out. My income tax!" - Nat King Cole

# DEBT

**DEBT IS WHEN YOU OWE SOMEONE MONEY**

## TYPES

### GOOD DEBTS

- Mortgages
- Home Equity Loans
- Lines of Credit
- School Loans
- Business Loan

### BAD DEBTS

- Credit Card Debt
- Auto Loans
- Loans from Questionable Sources (Payday Lenders)

## WHAT?

**CREDIT CARD**

Any time you don't pay in full, that's debt

**EMI**

Making payments for something you bought before

**PERSONAL LOAN**

Borrowed money from friends & relatives.

No matter how you package it, ***debt*** means you're at the ***mercy of someone else*** until you pay them back.

## HOW TO?

**WAYS TO HELP YOU MAKE FAST PROGRESS**

### AVALANCHE METHOD

Pay off debts with highest interest rates first

### SNOWBALL METHOD

Pay off smallest balances first

### PAYING OFF 20-YEARS LOAN IN 10 YEARS

1. Prepay one extra EMI per year and your loan will finish in 17 years.
2. Every year as your salary goes up, voluntarily increase your EMI by 10 per cent and your 20-year loan will be paid off in 10 years.

### HOW TO KEEP A TRACK OF DEBTS

1. Make a list of your loan accounts.
2. Sort the loan accounts in decreasing interest rates.
3. Plan to pay off the loans with higher interest rates first.

The amount of saving in interest cost may blow your mind.

# LIABILITY (DEBT) INFORMATION

| No. | BANK/ LENDER | DATE | LIABILITY TYPE | AMOUNT |
|---|---|---|---|---|
| 1 | | | | |
| 2 | | | | |
| 3 | | | | |
| 4 | | | | |
| 5 | | | | |
| 6 | | | | |
| 7 | | | | |
| 8 | | | | |
| 9 | | | | |
| 10 | | | | |
| 11 | | | | |
| 12 | | | | |
| 13 | | | | |
| 14 | | | | |
| 15 | | | | |
| 16 | | | | |
| 17 | | | | |
| 18 | | | | |
| 19 | | | | |
| 20 | | | | |
| 21 | | | | |
| 22 | | | | |
| 23 | | | | |
| 24 | | | | |
| 25 | | | | |

*Notes*

"Buying on the installment plan makes the months shorter and the years longer." - Anonymous

# LIABILITY (DEBT) INFORMATION

| No. | BANK/ LENDER | DATE | LIABILITY TYPE | AMOUNT |
|---|---|---|---|---|
| 1 | | | | |
| 2 | | | | |
| 3 | | | | |
| 4 | | | | |
| 5 | | | | |
| 6 | | | | |
| 7 | | | | |
| 8 | | | | |
| 9 | | | | |
| 10 | | | | |
| 11 | | | | |
| 12 | | | | |
| 13 | | | | |
| 14 | | | | |
| 15 | | | | |
| 16 | | | | |
| 17 | | | | |
| 18 | | | | |
| 19 | | | | |
| 20 | | | | |
| 21 | | | | |
| 22 | | | | |
| 23 | | | | |
| 24 | | | | |
| 25 | | | | |

*Notes*

A man with debt soon becomes a man with disturbance.

# LIABILITY (DEBT) INFORMATION

| No. | BANK/ LENDER | DATE | LIABILITY TYPE | AMOUNT |
|---|---|---|---|---|
| 1 | | | | |
| 2 | | | | |
| 3 | | | | |
| 4 | | | | |
| 5 | | | | |
| 6 | | | | |
| 7 | | | | |
| 8 | | | | |
| 9 | | | | |
| 10 | | | | |
| 11 | | | | |
| 12 | | | | |
| 13 | | | | |
| 14 | | | | |
| 15 | | | | |
| 16 | | | | |
| 17 | | | | |
| 18 | | | | |
| 19 | | | | |
| 20 | | | | |
| 21 | | | | |
| 22 | | | | |
| 23 | | | | |
| 24 | | | | |
| 25 | | | | |

*Notes*

"It is very iniquitous to make me pay debts, you have no idea, of the pain it gives one." - Lord Byron

# LIABILITY (DEBT) INFORMATION

| No. | BANK/ LENDER | DATE | LIABILITY TYPE | AMOUNT |
|---|---|---|---|---|
| 1 | | | | |
| 2 | | | | |
| 3 | | | | |
| 4 | | | | |
| 5 | | | | |
| 6 | | | | |
| 7 | | | | |
| 8 | | | | |
| 9 | | | | |
| 10 | | | | |
| 11 | | | | |
| 12 | | | | |
| 13 | | | | |
| 14 | | | | |
| 15 | | | | |
| 16 | | | | |
| 17 | | | | |
| 18 | | | | |
| 19 | | | | |
| 20 | | | | |
| 21 | | | | |
| 22 | | | | |
| 23 | | | | |
| 24 | | | | |
| 25 | | | | |

*Notes*

"A man with debt soon becomes a man with disturbance." - Anonymous

# MONEY LENDED (GIVEN) INFO

| No. | LOAN GIVEN TO | DATE ISSUE | AMOUNT | MODE OF PAY |
|---|---|---|---|---|
| 1 | | | | |
| 2 | | | | |
| 3 | | | | |
| 4 | | | | |
| 5 | | | | |
| 6 | | | | |
| 7 | | | | |
| 8 | | | | |
| 9 | | | | |
| 10 | | | | |
| 11 | | | | |
| 12 | | | | |
| 13 | | | | |
| 14 | | | | |
| 15 | | | | |
| 16 | | | | |
| 17 | | | | |
| 18 | | | | |
| 19 | | | | |
| 20 | | | | |
| 21 | | | | |
| 22 | | | | |
| 23 | | | | |
| 24 | | | | |
| 25 | | | | |

*Notes*

"If you want the time to pass quickly, just give your note for 90 days." - R.B. Thomas.

# MONEY LENDED (GIVEN) INFO

| DATE RETURN | TERMS & REMARKS |
|---|---|
| | |
| | |
| | |
| | |
| | |
| | |
| | |
| | |
| | |
| | |
| | |
| | |
| | |
| | |
| | |
| | |
| | |
| | |
| | |
| | |
| | |
| | |
| | |
| | |
| | |

*Notes*

"Debt is the secret foe of thrift, as vice and idleness are its open foes. The debt-habit is the twin brother of poverty."

- Anonymous

# DEBT PAID OFF INFORMATION

| No. | LENDER/BANKER | AMOUNT | CLEARANCE DATE | REMARKS |
|---|---|---|---|---|
| 1 | | | | |
| 2 | | | | |
| 3 | | | | |
| 4 | | | | |
| 5 | | | | |
| 6 | | | | |
| 7 | | | | |
| 8 | | | | |
| 9 | | | | |
| 10 | | | | |
| 11 | | | | |
| 12 | | | | |
| 13 | | | | |
| 14 | | | | |
| 15 | | | | |
| 16 | | | | |
| 17 | | | | |
| 18 | | | | |
| 19 | | | | |
| 20 | | | | |
| 21 | | | | |
| 22 | | | | |
| 23 | | | | |
| 24 | | | | |
| 25 | | | | |

*Notes*

The true freedom is when you have No-Debt!!

# DEBT PAID OFF INFORMATION

| No. | LENDER/BANKER | AMOUNT | CLEARANCE DATE | REMARKS |
|---|---|---|---|---|
| 1 | | | | |
| 2 | | | | |
| 3 | | | | |
| 4 | | | | |
| 5 | | | | |
| 6 | | | | |
| 7 | | | | |
| 8 | | | | |
| 9 | | | | |
| 10 | | | | |
| 11 | | | | |
| 12 | | | | |
| 13 | | | | |
| 14 | | | | |
| 15 | | | | |
| 16 | | | | |
| 17 | | | | |
| 18 | | | | |
| 19 | | | | |
| 20 | | | | |
| 21 | | | | |
| 22 | | | | |
| 23 | | | | |
| 24 | | | | |
| 25 | | | | |

*Notes*

With no debts, you can fully enjoy your paycheck without monthly payment burdens.

# HOME FUN EMI PAYMENT *tracker*

LENDER

INTEREST RATE

GOAL: PAY OFF DATE

START DATE

STARTING BALANCE

1 BRICK=1 MONTH EMI

## HOME LOAN PAY-OFF

| No. | YEAR | JAN | FEB | MAR | APR | MAY | JUNE | JULY | AUG | SEP | OCT | NOV | DEC |
|---|---|---|---|---|---|---|---|---|---|---|---|---|---|
| 1 | | | | | | | | | | | | | |
| 2 | | | | | | | | | | | | | |
| 3 | | | | | | | | | | | | | |
| 4 | | | | | | | | | | | | | |
| 5 | | | | | | | | | | | | | |
| 6 | | | | | | | | | | | | | |
| 7 | | | | | | | | | | | | | |
| 8 | | | | | | | | | | | | | |
| 9 | | | | | | | | | | | | | |
| 10 | | | | | | | | | | | | | |
| 11 | | | | | | | | | | | | | |
| 12 | | | | | | | | | | | | | |
| 13 | | | | | | | | | | | | | |
| 14 | | | | | | | | | | | | | |
| 15 | | | | | | | | | | | | | |

**15 YEARS TRACKING**

**Color Each brick each month you pay the EMI. It gives sense of achievement & is a visual treat to track your progress.**

"I will forever believe that buying a home is a great investment. Why? Because you can't live in a stock certificate. You can't live in a mutual fund." - Oprah Winfrey.

# HOME FUN EMI PAYMENT *tracker*

LENDER

INTEREST RATE

GOAL: PAY OFF DATE

START DATE

STARTING BALANCE

1 BRICK=1 MONTH EMI

## HOME LOAN PAY-OFF

| No. | YEAR | JAN | FEB | MAR | APR | MAY | JUNE | JULY | AUG | SEP | OCT | NOV | DEC |
|---|---|---|---|---|---|---|---|---|---|---|---|---|---|
| 1 | | | | | | | | | | | | | |
| 2 | | | | | | | | | | | | | |
| 3 | | | | | | | | | | | | | |
| 4 | | | | | | | | | | | | | |
| 5 | | | | | | | | | | | | | |
| 6 | | | | | | | | | | | | | |
| 7 | | | | | | | | | | | | | |
| 8 | | | | | | | | | | | | | |
| 9 | | | | | | | | | | | | | |
| 10 | | | | | | | | | | | | | |
| 11 | | | | | | | | | | | | | |
| 12 | | | | | | | | | | | | | |
| 13 | | | | | | | | | | | | | |
| 14 | | | | | | | | | | | | | |
| 15 | | | | | | | | | | | | | |
| 16 | | | | | | | | | | | | | |
| 17 | | | | | | | | | | | | | |
| 18 | | | | | | | | | | | | | |
| 19 | | | | | | | | | | | | | |
| 20 | | | | | | | | | | | | | |

**20 YEARS TRACKING**

**Color Each brick each month you pay the EMI. It gives sense of achievement & is a visual treat to track your progress**

"Buying real estate is not only the best way, the quickest way, the safest way, but the only way to become wealthy." - Marshall Field.

# HOME EMI PAYMENT
## Tracker

LENDER

INTEREST

ORIGINAL LOAN PERIOD

LOAN ACCOUNT NO#:

LOAN AMOUNT

DATE OF 1ST PAYMENT

START EMI

DOWNPAYMENT

| DATE | STARTING AMT | PAYMENT | INTEREST | PRINCIPAL | BALANCE |
|---|---|---|---|---|---|
| | | | | | |
| | | | | | |
| | | | | | |
| | | | | | |
| | | | | | |
| | | | | | |
| | | | | | |
| | | | | | |
| | | | | | |
| | | | | | |
| | | | | | |
| | | | | | |
| | | | | | |
| | | | | | |
| | | | | | |
| | | | | | |

| DATE | STARTING BALANCE | PAYMENT | INTEREST | PRINCIPAL | REMAINING BALANCE |
|---|---|---|---|---|---|
| | | | | | |
| | | | | | |
| | | | | | |
| | | | | | |
| | | | | | |
| | | | | | |
| | | | | | |
| | | | | | |
| | | | | | |
| | | | | | |
| | | | | | |
| | | | | | |
| | | | | | |
| | | | | | |
| | | | | | |
| | | | | | |
| | | | | | |
| | | | | | |
| | | | | | |

"Twenty years from now, you will be more disappointed by the things you didn't do than by the ones you did do. So throw off the bowlines. Sail away from the safe harbor. Catch the trade winds in your sails. Explore. Dream. Discover." - Mark Twain

# CAR LOAN PAY-OFF

| CREDITOR | AMOUNT TO PAY | START DATE | INTEREST RATE |
|---|---|---|---|
| | | | |

*Notes*

Color the car as soon as you clear that month's EMI. Below the car is the box where you can write your EMI amount or date paid on.

# CAR LOAN PAY-OFF

| CREDITOR | AMOUNT TO PAY | START DATE | INTEREST RATE |
|---|---|---|---|
| | | | |

| DATE | STARTING BALANCE | PAYMENT | CLOSING BALANCE |
|---|---|---|---|
| | | | |
| | | | |
| | | | |
| | | | |
| | | | |
| | | | |
| | | | |
| | | | |
| | | | |
| | | | |
| | | | |
| | | | |
| | | | |
| | | | |
| | | | |
| | | | |
| | | | |

*Notes*

..............................................................................................................

..............................................................................................................

..............................................................................................................

"If you think nobody cares if you're alive, try missing a couple of car payments." - Earl Wilson

# DEBT SNOWBALL TRACKER

MONTH /YEAR

CREDITOR | ACCOUNT

AMOUNT | DUE DATE | INTEREST RATE

GOAL PAYOFF DATE | MINIMUM PAYMENT

| DATE | PAID AMOUNT | BALANCE | NOTES |
|---|---|---|---|
| | | | |
| | | | |
| | | | |
| | | | |
| | | | |
| | | | |
| | | | |
| | | | |
| | | | |
| | | | |
| | | | |
| | | | |
| | | | |
| | | | |
| | | | |
| | | | |
| | | | |
| | | | |
| | | | |

**VISUAL PAYOFF PROGRESS**

| % | ₹ |
|---|---|
| 100% | ₹ |
| 95% | ₹ |
| 90% | ₹ |
| 85% | ₹ |
| 80% | ₹ |
| 75% | ₹ |
| 70% | ₹ |
| 65% | ₹ |
| 60% | ₹ |
| 55% | ₹ |
| 50% | ₹ |
| 45% | ₹ |
| 40% | ₹ |
| 35% | ₹ |
| 30% | ₹ |
| 25% | ₹ |
| 20% | ₹ |
| 15% | ₹ |
| 10% | ₹ |
| 5% | ₹ |
| 0% | ₹ |

"A man under debt not only loses the peace but also the people."
- Anonymous

# DEBT SNOWBALL TRACKER

MONTH /YEAR

CREDITOR | ACCOUNT

AMOUNT | DUE DATE | INTEREST RATE

GOAL PAYOFF DATE | MINIMUM PAYMENT

| DATE | PAID AMOUNT | BALANCE | NOTES |
|---|---|---|---|
| | | | |
| | | | |
| | | | |
| | | | |
| | | | |
| | | | |
| | | | |
| | | | |
| | | | |
| | | | |
| | | | |
| | | | |
| | | | |
| | | | |
| | | | |
| | | | |
| | | | |
| | | | |
| | | | |

**VISUAL PAYOFF PROGRESS**

100% ₹
95% ₹
90% ₹
85% ₹
80% ₹
75% ₹
70% ₹
65% ₹
60% ₹
55% ₹
50% ₹
45% ₹
40% ₹
35% ₹
30% ₹
25% ₹
20% ₹
15% ₹
10% ₹
5% ₹
0% ₹

"Owing money has never concerned me so long as I know where it could be repaid." – Col. Henry Crown

# DEBT TRACKER

**SOURCE:**
**DEBT :**
**BALANCE :**
**ADV. PAYMENT :**

| DATE | PAYMENT | BALANCE |
|---|---|---|
| | | |
| | | |
| | | |
| | | |
| | | |
| | | |
| | | |
| | | |
| | | |
| | | |
| | | |
| | | |

**SOURCE:**
**DEBT :**
**BALANCE :**
**ADV. PAYMENT :**

| DATE | PAYMENT | BALANCE |
|---|---|---|
| | | |
| | | |
| | | |
| | | |
| | | |
| | | |
| | | |
| | | |
| | | |
| | | |
| | | |
| | | |

**SOURCE:**
**DEBT :**
**BALANCE :**
**ADV. PAYMENT :**

| DATE | PAYMENT | BALANCE |
|---|---|---|
| | | |
| | | |
| | | |
| | | |
| | | |
| | | |
| | | |
| | | |
| | | |
| | | |
| | | |
| | | |

**SOURCE:**
**DEBT :**
**BALANCE :**
**ADV. PAYMENT :**

| DATE | PAYMENT | BALANCE |
|---|---|---|
| | | |
| | | |
| | | |
| | | |
| | | |
| | | |
| | | |
| | | |
| | | |
| | | |
| | | |
| | | |

"A liability is anything that causes you to spend money and results in net value decreases." - Hendrith Smith

# DEBT TRACKER

**SOURCE:**
**DEBT :**
**BALANCE :**
**ADV. PAYMENT :**

| DATE | PAYMENT | BALANCE |
|---|---|---|
| | | |
| | | |
| | | |
| | | |
| | | |
| | | |
| | | |
| | | |
| | | |
| | | |
| | | |
| | | |

**SOURCE:**
**DEBT :**
**BALANCE :**
**ADV. PAYMENT :**

| DATE | PAYMENT | BALANCE |
|---|---|---|
| | | |
| | | |
| | | |
| | | |
| | | |
| | | |
| | | |
| | | |
| | | |
| | | |
| | | |
| | | |

**SOURCE:**
**DEBT :**
**BALANCE :**
**ADV. PAYMENT :**

| DATE | PAYMENT | BALANCE |
|---|---|---|
| | | |
| | | |
| | | |
| | | |
| | | |
| | | |
| | | |
| | | |
| | | |
| | | |
| | | |
| | | |

**SOURCE:**
**DEBT :**
**BALANCE :**
**ADV. PAYMENT :**

| DATE | PAYMENT | BALANCE |
|---|---|---|
| | | |
| | | |
| | | |
| | | |
| | | |
| | | |
| | | |
| | | |
| | | |
| | | |
| | | |
| | | |

"Debt is the slavery of the free." - Publilius Syrus

# DEBT TRACKER

SOURCE:
DEBT :
BALANCE :
ADV. PAYMENT :

| DATE | PAYMENT | BALANCE |
|---|---|---|
| | | |
| | | |
| | | |
| | | |
| | | |
| | | |
| | | |
| | | |
| | | |
| | | |
| | | |
| | | |

SOURCE:
DEBT :
BALANCE :
ADV. PAYMENT :

| DATE | PAYMENT | BALANCE |
|---|---|---|
| | | |
| | | |
| | | |
| | | |
| | | |
| | | |
| | | |
| | | |
| | | |
| | | |
| | | |
| | | |

SOURCE:
DEBT :
BALANCE :
ADV. PAYMENT :

| DATE | PAYMENT | BALANCE |
|---|---|---|
| | | |
| | | |
| | | |
| | | |
| | | |
| | | |
| | | |
| | | |
| | | |
| | | |
| | | |
| | | |

SOURCE:
DEBT :
BALANCE :
ADV. PAYMENT :

| DATE | PAYMENT | BALANCE |
|---|---|---|
| | | |
| | | |
| | | |
| | | |
| | | |
| | | |
| | | |
| | | |
| | | |
| | | |
| | | |
| | | |

"Let us live is as small a circle as we will, we are either debtors or creditors before we have had time look around." - Johann Wolfgang

# DEBT TRACKER

**SOURCE:**
**DEBT :**
**BALANCE :**
**ADV. PAYMENT :**

| DATE | PAYMENT | BALANCE |
|---|---|---|
| | | |
| | | |
| | | |
| | | |
| | | |
| | | |
| | | |
| | | |
| | | |
| | | |
| | | |
| | | |

**SOURCE:**
**DEBT :**
**BALANCE :**
**ADV. PAYMENT :**

| DATE | PAYMENT | BALANCE |
|---|---|---|
| | | |
| | | |
| | | |
| | | |
| | | |
| | | |
| | | |
| | | |
| | | |
| | | |
| | | |
| | | |

**SOURCE:**
**DEBT :**
**BALANCE :**
**ADV. PAYMENT :**

| DATE | PAYMENT | BALANCE |
|---|---|---|
| | | |
| | | |
| | | |
| | | |
| | | |
| | | |
| | | |
| | | |
| | | |
| | | |
| | | |
| | | |

**SOURCE:**
**DEBT :**
**BALANCE :**
**ADV. PAYMENT :**

| DATE | PAYMENT | BALANCE |
|---|---|---|
| | | |
| | | |
| | | |
| | | |
| | | |
| | | |
| | | |
| | | |
| | | |
| | | |
| | | |
| | | |

"There are four things every person has more of than they know: sins, debt, years, and foes." - Persian Proverb

# LENDING TRACKER

**DEBT GIVEN TO :**

**AMOUNT GIVEN :**

**DATE :**

**TERMS OF RETURN:**

| DATE | PAYMENT | BALANCE |
|---|---|---|
| | | |
| | | |
| | | |
| | | |
| | | |
| | | |
| | | |
| | | |
| | | |
| | | |
| | | |
| | | |

**DEBT GIVEN TO :**

**AMOUNT GIVEN:**

**DATE :**

**TERMS OF RETURN:**

| DATE | PAYMENT | BALANCE |
|---|---|---|
| | | |
| | | |
| | | |
| | | |
| | | |
| | | |
| | | |
| | | |
| | | |
| | | |
| | | |
| | | |

**DEBT GIVEN TO :**

**AMOUNT GIVEN :**

**DATE:**

**TERMS OF RETURN:**

| DATE | PAYMENT | BALANCE |
|---|---|---|
| | | |
| | | |
| | | |
| | | |
| | | |
| | | |
| | | |
| | | |
| | | |
| | | |
| | | |
| | | |

**DEBT GIVEN TO :**

**AMOUNT GIVEN:**

**DATE :**

**TERMS OF RETURN:**

| DATE | PAYMENT | BALANCE |
|---|---|---|
| | | |
| | | |
| | | |
| | | |
| | | |
| | | |
| | | |
| | | |
| | | |
| | | |
| | | |
| | | |

"Debt can turn a free, happy person into a bitter human being." - Michael Mihalik

# LENDING TRACKER

**DEBT GIVEN TO :**

**AMOUNT GIVEN :**

**DATE:**

**TERMS OF RETURN:**

| DATE | PAYMENT | BALANCE |
|---|---|---|
| | | |
| | | |
| | | |
| | | |
| | | |
| | | |
| | | |
| | | |
| | | |
| | | |
| | | |
| | | |

**DEBT GIVEN TO :**

**AMOUNT GIVEN:**

**DATE :**

**TERMS OF RETURN:**

| DATE | PAYMENT | BALANCE |
|---|---|---|
| | | |
| | | |
| | | |
| | | |
| | | |
| | | |
| | | |
| | | |
| | | |
| | | |
| | | |
| | | |

**DEBT GIVEN TO :**

**AMOUNT GIVEN :**

**DATE OF LOAN GIVEN :**

**TERMS OF RETURN:**

| DATE | PAYMENT | BALANCE |
|---|---|---|
| | | |
| | | |
| | | |
| | | |
| | | |
| | | |
| | | |
| | | |
| | | |
| | | |
| | | |
| | | |

**DEBT GIVEN TO :**

**AMOUNT GIVEN:**

**DATE OF LOAN GIVEN:**

**TERMS OF RETURN:**

| DATE | PAYMENT | BALANCE |
|---|---|---|
| | | |
| | | |
| | | |
| | | |
| | | |
| | | |
| | | |
| | | |
| | | |
| | | |
| | | |
| | | |

"Buying on the installment plan makes the months shorter and the years longer." - Unknown

# STUDENT LOAN PAYMENT TRACKER

| CREDITOR | AMOUNT TO PAY | START DATE | INTEREST RATE |
| --- | --- | --- | --- |
| | | | |

| DATE | STARTING BALANCE | PAYMENT | CLOSING BALANCE |
| --- | --- | --- | --- |
| | | | |
| | | | |
| | | | |
| | | | |
| | | | |
| | | | |
| | | | |
| | | | |
| | | | |
| | | | |
| | | | |
| | | | |
| | | | |
| | | | |
| | | | |
| | | | |
| | | | |
| | | | |

*Notes*

.......................................................................................................................

.......................................................................................................................

.......................................................................................................................

# STUDENT LOAN PAYMENT TRACKER

| CREDITOR | AMOUNT TO PAY | START DATE | INTEREST RATE |
|---|---|---|---|
| | | | |

| DATE | STARTING BALANCE | PAYMENT | CLOSING BALANCE |
|---|---|---|---|
| | | | |
| | | | |
| | | | |
| | | | |
| | | | |
| | | | |
| | | | |
| | | | |
| | | | |
| | | | |
| | | | |
| | | | |
| | | | |
| | | | |
| | | | |
| | | | |
| | | | |
| | | | |
| | | | |

*Notes*

# DEBT REPAYMENT TRACKER

**DUE DATE:**

**STARTING BALANCE:**

**INTEREST RATE:**

**MIN. PAYMENT AMOUNT:**

**GOAL PAYMENT AMOUNT:**

**GOAL PAYOFF DATE:**

## REPAYMENT TRACKER

| DATE | STARTING BALANCE | REPAYMENT AMOUNT | ENDING BALANCE |
|---|---|---|---|
| | | | |
| | | | |
| | | | |
| | | | |
| | | | |
| | | | |
| | | | |
| | | | |
| | | | |
| | | | |
| | | | |
| | | | |
| | | | |
| | | | |
| | | | |
| | | | |
| | | | |
| | | | |

| DATE | STARTING BALANCE | REPAYMENT AMOUNT | ENDING BALANCE |
|---|---|---|---|
| | | | |
| | | | |
| | | | |
| | | | |
| | | | |
| | | | |
| | | | |
| | | | |
| | | | |
| | | | |
| | | | |
| | | | |
| | | | |
| | | | |
| | | | |
| | | | |
| | | | |
| | | | |

"Debt can turn a free, happy person into a bitter human being." - Michael Mihalik.

# DEBT REPAYMENT TRACKER

**DUE DATE:**

**STARTING BALANCE:**

**INTEREST RATE:**

**MIN. PAYMENT AMOUNT:**

**GOAL PAYMENT AMOUNT:**

**GOAL PAYOFF DATE:**

## REPAYMENT TRACKER

| DATE | STARTING BALANCE | REPAYMENT AMOUNT | ENDING BALANCE |
|---|---|---|---|
| | | | |
| | | | |
| | | | |
| | | | |
| | | | |
| | | | |
| | | | |
| | | | |
| | | | |
| | | | |
| | | | |
| | | | |
| | | | |
| | | | |
| | | | |
| | | | |
| | | | |
| | | | |

| DATE | STARTING BALANCE | REPAYMENT AMOUNT | ENDING BALANCE |
|---|---|---|---|
| | | | |
| | | | |
| | | | |
| | | | |
| | | | |
| | | | |
| | | | |
| | | | |
| | | | |
| | | | |
| | | | |
| | | | |
| | | | |
| | | | |
| | | | |
| | | | |
| | | | |
| | | | |

"Good times are when people make debts to pay in bad times." - Robert Quillen.

# RETIREMENT

# WHAT IS THE FIRE MOVEMENT?

## Financial Independence, Retire Early

### COAST FIRE

You have enough saved (with the power of compounding) to cover traditional retirement. This is a fairly low number to hit when you are in your 20s or 30s since time is on your side..

### LEAN FIRE

The minimum amount of money required to sustain after retirement. One need to maintain a strict and frugal budget.

### BARISTA FIRE

- It's a movement where you still save aggressively towards retirement, but instead of quitting work full stop and living off of your investments, you save until you reach the point where you only need to work part-time (or earn some passive income).

### TRADITIONAL FIRE

- Live off withdrawals from your investment portfolio for the rest of your life.

### FAT FIRE

- This is for the individual with a traditional lifestyle who aims to save substantially more than the average worker but doesn't want to reduce their current standard of living.
- Aggressive saving & investment strategies is needed.

# RETIREMENT INVESTMENTS

NATIONAL PENSION SCHEME

PUBLIC PROVIDENT FUND

ATAL BIHARI YOJNA

STOCK MARKET INVESTMENT

REAL ESTATE YIELD

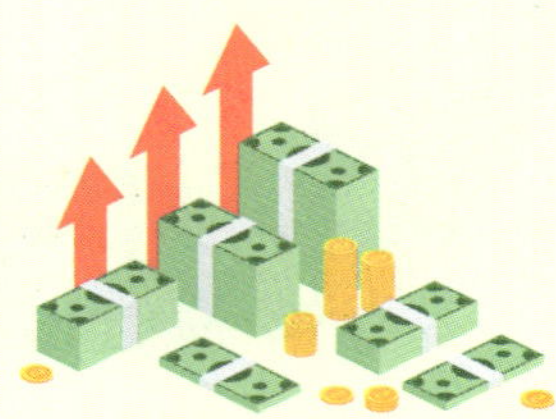

LONG TERM MUTUAL FUND INVESTMENT

BUSINESS PROFITS/INCOME

LONG TERM FD/BOND, ETC.

# CALCULATING RETIREMENT FIRE

| PARTICULARS | VALUE (INR) | FORMULAE |
|---|---|---|
| Desired monthly expenses (today) | | A |
| Current age | | B |
| Retirement age | | C |
| Inflation rate (%) | | D |
| | | |
| Yearly expenses (today) | | A*12=E |
| Yearly expenses (retirement age) | | F= E*(100+D) ^ (C-B) |
| | | |
| Lean FIRE | | F*20 |
| FIRE | | F*25 |
| FAT FIRE | | F*50 |

# RETIREMENT GOALS

Think about each of these areas of your life through an old person's lens. Picture your daily life and what you hope to be doing each day.
Do you want to relive your lost hobby, learn new things, help your grandkids or travel?
Make your plan below so you can retire with intention.

| FAMILY | FRIEND |
| --- | --- |
| | |

| SPIRITUALTY | SELF-CARE |
| --- | --- |
| | |

| WORK | COMMUNITY |
| --- | --- |
| | |

| WEALTH | TRAVEL |
| --- | --- |
| | |

| OVERALL LIFE |
| --- |
| |

# RETIREMENT CHECKLIST

- **Plan your ideal retirement lifestyle**
- **Estimate Lumpsum required to fund lifestyle**
- **Calculate the value of asset you aim to have**
- **Calculate how much income assets will create**
- **Calculate weekly monthly retirement savings figure and put it into your budget**
- **Adjust your budget for old age expense**
- **Setup automatic savings account for retirement do not touch it**
- **Investigate free money you are entitled to (Provident Fund, Gratuity, Policy)**
- **Review your retirement funds, fees, and returns.**
- **Consider risks & plan accordingly (outliving inflation, share market crash, changes in retirement tax laws etc.)**
- **Review & adjust annually**

# RETIREMENT BUCKET LIST

## Notes

# NOMINEE

## WHAT?

A nominee is someone appointed by the asset holder to receive the assets in case of their demise.

**NOMINEE APPOINTED BY ASSET HOLDER**

=

**CUSTODIAN: GAURDS, PROTECTS OR MAINTAINS THE ASSETS**

≠

**NOT A LEGAL OWNER**

**Nominees act as custodians of the assets but do not have legal ownership rights**

## WHY?

So you might be wondering if the nominee is not the sole owner, why does such a concept exist in the first place?

**After your passing**

**Funds invested in insurance, mutual funds, or stocks get neglected.**

**These funds, if unclaimed for years, go to unclaimed account.**

### WITHOUT A NOMINATION

Legal heirs must provide death certificates and proof of relation to claim assets from entities like insurance companies, mutual funds, shares, and real estate, which can be time-consuming.

### WITH NOMINATION

If nominated, funds will go to someone you trust, and who can further help, in process of passing it to your legal heirs.

**So, to simplify, if a nominee exists, such hassles are avoided since the company is bound to transfer all your money or assets to the nominee.**

Understand the difference between legal heirs and nominees in financial planning in India. Seek advice from your legal experts to ensure nominations align with your financial planning for a seamless asset transfer to loved ones.

# DOES NOMINATION REALLY HELP?

## FACT

### UNCLAIMED ACCOUNT

As per RBI, deposit accounts which were not operated for 10 years or more are ***unclaimed account***. State Bank of India (SBI) is on top in terms of unclaimed deposits with Rs 8,086 crore in the year 2024.

**UNCLAIMED ACCOUNT** = 

**ACCOUNT UNTOUCHED FOR MORE THAN 10 YEARS**

According to information presented in Parliament on December 19, there were ₹42,270 crore in total unclaimed bank deposits in the fiscal year 2023—a 28 percent increase over the same period the previous year.

## REASON

- **WRONG INFO OF NOMINEE REGISTERED**
- **NOMINEE PREDECEASES THE NOMINATOR**
- **NOMINEE IS UNAWARE OF THE ACCOUNT**

## SOLUTION

- **CREATE A WILL**
- **CREATE A TRUST (OPTIONAL)**
- **DISCUSS YOUR FINANCES WITH SPOUSE OR A TRUSTED FAMILY MEMBER**
- **APPOINT AN ADVOCATE TO READ OUT YOUR WILL AND ASSETS IN YOUR ABSENCE**

# RETIREMENT FUND TRACKER

**ACCOUNT DETAILS**

| ACCOUNT HOLDER: | TYPE OF RETIREMENT: |
|---|---|

| DATE | CONTRIBUTION SOURCE | BALANCE | NOTES |
|---|---|---|---|
| | | | |
| | | | |
| | | | |
| | | | |
| | | | |
| | | | |
| | | | |
| | | | |
| | | | |
| | | | |
| | | | |
| | | | |
| | | | |
| | | | |
| | | | |
| | | | |
| | | | |
| | | | |
| | | | |
| | | | |
| | | | |
| | | | |
| | | | |

# RETIREMENT FUND TRACKER

**ACCOUNT DETAILS**

| ACCOUNT HOLDER: | TYPE OF RETIREMENT: |
|---|---|

| DATE | CONTRIBUTION SOURCE | BALANCE | NOTES |
|---|---|---|---|
| | | | |
| | | | |
| | | | |
| | | | |
| | | | |
| | | | |
| | | | |
| | | | |
| | | | |
| | | | |
| | | | |
| | | | |
| | | | |
| | | | |
| | | | |
| | | | |
| | | | |
| | | | |
| | | | |
| | | | |
| | | | |
| | | | |
| | | | |

# RETIREMENT ACCOUNT INFORMATION

**ACCOUNT DETAILS**

COMPANY:

TYPE OF RETIREMENT:

ACCOUNT /WEBSITE:

ACCOUNT NUMBER:

USERNAME:

CURRENT VALUE:

**NOTES**

**ACCOUNT DETAILS**

COMPANY:

TYPE OF RETIREMENT:

ACCOUNT /WEBSITE:

ACCOUNT NUMBER:

USERNAME:

CURRENT VALUE:

**NOTES**

# RETIREMENT ACCOUNT INFORMATION

**ACCOUNT DETAILS**

COMPANY:

TYPE OF RETIREMENT:

ACCOUNT /WEBSITE:

ACCOUNT NUMBER:

USERNAME:

CURRENT VALUE:

**NOTES**

**ACCOUNT DETAILS**

COMPANY:

TYPE OF RETIREMENT:

ACCOUNT /WEBSITE:

ACCOUNT NUMBER:

USERNAME:

CURRENT VALUE:

**NOTES**

# LEGAL HEIR & BENEFICIARY

## LEGAL HEIR

Entitled to inherit

under the law of succession

Comes into play when there is no will.

Legal heirs are typically close relatives such as children, spouses, or parents

## BENEFICIARY

An individual named in a legal document such as a will or insurance policy

Receives assets or property

Beneficiaries can be relatives, friends, organizations, or even charities

A legal heir's claim to an estate is determined by their relationship to the deceased and applicable laws, while a beneficiary's claim is based on the deceased's expressed wishes in a legal document. It is possible for an individual to be both a legal heir and a beneficiary.

## INDIAN LAW

There are two ways to succeed in a property that a successor must understand and have knowledge about. These are:

1. **Intestate Succession:** This means that the ***deceased person did not leave any will*** behind, so the property and assets are equally divided and distributed among heirs.
2. **Through Will / Testamentary Succession:** This means that the deceased person leaves behind a Will, which is of legal value, and property is distributed as it is mentioned in the Will as per laws of inheritance.

***The Indian laws of inheritance govern the division, distribution, and protection of the property and assets*** of a deceased person in two cases which are divided as:

- **Hindu Succession Act, 1956**
- **Indian Succession Act, 1925**
- **Muslim Personal Law**

These laws are designed to respect the diverse religious practices and provide a legal framework for the orderly succession of property.

It's important to note that the presence of a will generally takes precedence over personal law, provided it complies with all legal requirements.

If you need more detailed information, it's advisable to consult with a legal expert.

# WILL

## WHAT?

**LEGAL DOCUMENT**

**DIRECTS WHO GETS YOUR STUFF AFTER YOU ARE DECEASED**

**Distribute Assets**

**Charity Donations**

**Children Guardian**

**Burial Instructions**

## TYPES

**TESTAMENTARY**

Written & Witnessed

**ORAL**

Spoken But Not Written

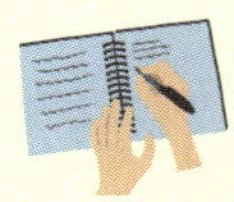

**HOLOGRAPHIC**

Handwritten Without Witnesses

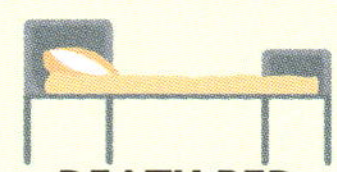

**DEATH BED**

Hard to Enforce

## HOW TO CREATE :

**CHOOSE AN EXECUTOR**

the person who administers a person's estate upon their death

**CREATE WITH AN ONLINE TEMPLATE OR AN ADVOCATE**

Study your requirements and download the template accordingly. It is best to visit your lawyer.

**SIGN WITH WITNESS AND GET NOTARIZED**

Without notary, will is valid in India but **2 witnesses' signature is a MUST.**

**TELL FRIENDS & FAMILY WHERE TO FIND IT!**

Tell your spouse or trusted person in your family or friends.

# WILL FORMAT

I ______________________________ age _______years, a _______(female/male) Indian Inhabitant, residing at ____________________________________________
I do hereby revoke all my former will, codicils or other Testamentary dispositions and hereby declare this to be my last will and Testament made at Mumbai this
Date ______day of Month ___________, Year ___________

1. I am maintaining good health, and I am possessed of sound mind. This will is made by me of my own independent decision and free violation and in perfectly sound health and sound mind, I have not been influences, cajoled or coerced by any person.
2. My family consist of the following members:
   i. ________________________________________
   ii. ________________________________________
   iii. ________________________________________
   iv. ________________________________________
   v. ________________________________________
   vi. ________________________________________

3. I have during my lifetime acquired properties and I am possessed of assets in the shape of Movable and Immovable Properties and chooses in action. Keeping in view the dissentions in the family and possible disputes, which may arise relating to inheritance opening out at my demise and in order to save the assets from unnecessary litigation amongst my relatives and others. I so here by devise and declare all the estate which I am holding at present/or which I may acquire in future in the manner as mentioned herein below.

4. I hereby appoint my husband/wife namely ______________the Executor of this my Last will in case my wife__________________ predeceases me then my son/daughter __________________ will be executor of my this will.

5. I direct that the said Executor shall pay my funeral and other expenses for obsequies ceremonies, just debts, taxes and other liabilities, out of the property that I have at the time of my death and the balance of my total properties shall be bequeathed.

6. I devise and bequeath all my Immovable and Movable Properties to my wife __________ and she will be owner for her lifetime and will be able to make her will as her desire.
7. In case my wife __________ predeceases me then all my Immovable and Movable property will be bequeathed as follows:

**(A) IMMOVABLE PROPERTIES**
All my immovable property will be bequeathed to my child namely __________

**(B) MOVABLE PROPERTIES**
i) Rs. ______ to be given to my daughter namely__________
ii) Rs.__________ to given to my granddaughter i.e son's daughter.
iii) Rs.__________ to be given to my grandson i.e my daughter's son and after above amounts are paid whatsoever left including any assets which I may acquire in future, or I may dispose of Some Assets will be given to my son __________

Signed by the within named Testatrix)
______________________________)
Acknowledged by her as her last will and) Testament in the presence of each have)

WITNESSES:
1. ______________________________
2. ______________________________

**NOTE:**

1. This is a ***specimen format*** provided for ***information purpose only***. To be suitably modifies as per requirement.
2. All the pages of will including schedules to be signed.
3. Signature of ***two witness is a must.***
4. The will can be registered or unregistered. The ***advantage of registered will*** is that in case of disputes, it can be proved easily.
5. The will deed can be made out on plain paper.
6. Will registration ***cost will be very less***.
7. The original copy of the executed will can be kept in a safe and secured place.
8. Having ***a valid Will simplifies asset distribution***, but without one, unclaimed assets can result in significant losses.
9. Please ***refer to the Indian Law Page in this book***, for detail understanding.
10. ***Visit the Lawyer for execution and indepth knowledge on this topic.***

Will sample taken randomly from google.com

# My Notes

# Notes

Date:

# *Notes*

Date:

# *Notes*

Date:

*Notes*

Date:

## Notes

Date:

# Notes

Date:

# Brain Dump!!

# Brain Dump!!

# Brain Dump!!

# Brain Dump!!

# Brain Dump!!

# Brain Dump!!

# Brain Dump!!

# Brain Dump!!